For the last 11 years, the author has been a professor of Public Policy at the Batten School of Leadership and Public Policy at the University of Virginia. Prior to this, he was the executive director of the National Governors Association (NGA) for 28 years. This bi-partisan organization represents the nation's governors and state governments on domestic policy issues that come before the U.S. Congress. Prior to NGA, he worked for seven years at the non-partisan U.S. Congressional Budget Office, serving the last two years as the Deputy Director.

He has written numerous professional articles and authored or co-authored four public policy books. The author received his master's and Ph.D. degrees in economics from the University of Connecticut.

This book is dedicated to the students in my previous capstone classes at the University of Virginia who worked hard to develop rigorous analytical frameworks as the foundation for their papers.

Raymond Scheppach

A Guide to Writing a Capstone Public Policy Report

AUSTIN MACAULEY PUBLISHERS™

LONDON • CAMBRIDGE • NEW YORK • SHARJAH

Ordering Information
Quantity sales: Special discounts are available on quantity purchases by corporations, associations, and others. For details, contact the publisher at the address below.

Publisher's Cataloging-in-Publication data
Scheppach, Raymond
A Guide to Writing a Capstone Public Policy Report

ISBN 9798886939385 (Paperback)
ISBN 9798886939392 (ePub e-book)

Library of Congress Control Number: 2023918655

www.austinmacauley.com/us

First Published 2024
Austin Macauley Publishers LLC
40 Wall Street, 33rd Floor, Suite 3302
New York, NY 10005
USA

mail-usa@austinmacauley.com
+1 (646) 5125767

I would like to thank Eric Patashnik, previously a professor at the University of Virginia and currently at Brown University, for assisting me in teaching the capstone class the first several years. Our many conversations were very helpful in creating the outline of this book.

Second, I would like to thank Erica Fitzpatrick of Church Street Editorial for not only editing the manuscript but, more importantly, indicating places where more research was needed. Finally, I would like to thank Maxwell Halbruner, a former student at the University of Virginia, for gathering data and calculating various metrics.

Table of Contents

Preface

I have been fortunate to teach the capstone course for students in the Master of Public Policy (MPP) program at the University of Virginia (UVA) Frank Batten School of Leadership and Public Policy for more than 10 years. Before joining the faculty of UVA, I spent 35 years working on both federal and state public policy issues in the Congressional Budget Office and for the nation's governors as the executive director of the National Governors Association (NGA). The NGA is at the critical nexus between state and federal domestic policy. This nexus is key. Except for Social Security and Medicare—and perhaps national parks and forests—states administer all domestic programs. The programs may be authorized and partially or totally funded by the federal government, but they are operated at the state level. I value the learning experience I gained working with political leaders from federal and state governments on major domestic policy issues such as welfare reform and the Patient Protection and Affordable Care Act.

In talking to and observing students over this 10-year period, I have found that their greatest challenge is translating the concepts described in books on cost-benefit and cost-effectiveness analysis into performing that analysis, and then writing a report. The first goal of this book is to fill this void by providing detailed steps on how to quantify various measures, with illustrative examples.

A second goal of this book is to help students write an analytical, not a descriptive, paper. The foundation of an analytical paper is a problem statement that defines the public policy issue and the outcome definition that must be consistent with the problem statement. Next, the writer must establish metrics for the various criteria so that the evaluations are rigorous. Finally, cost-effectiveness must be calculated correctly. In the political world, cost is the major driver of policy decisions, and so this part of the analysis is critical.

A third goal is to integrate financing into the discussion of federal and state policy. Too often, students talk about policy as though it were one decision. It is not: Authorizations and appropriations generally go through different committees at different times. Many authorizations never receive an appropriation and thus never become operational. Exceptions to this statement exist for entitlements, such as Social Security and Medicare, where the authorizing language automatically creates spending authority, and certain other mandatory spending programs such as farm support programs. Most times, however, particularly at the state and local government levels, where entitlements are rare, there are two different actions-authorization and then appropriation. Both steps are important, but each raises multiple political and implementation issues.

A fourth goal is to bring political realities into the discussion. Political calculations often dominate policy, and we need to recognize this reality.

A fifth goal of this book is to heighten the focus on policy implementation, a subject generally given short shrift in most policy books, even though more policies fail because of poor implementation than because of improper conceptualization.

Students often initially want to evaluate federal policies. However, state and local governments, even school districts, have more policy levers. Students can often study policies at these levels of government in more depth, which in the end they may find more satisfying. State and local projects also often have sponsors with more passion and interest in the analysis.

Raymond Scheppach
Charlottesville, Virginia
June,2023

Chapter 1
Introduction

Many schools of public policy require their students to write a capstone or master's thesis as the culmination of their academic work. This document is a requirement for graduation, and students often use it as an example of their work when applying for jobs. It is also an opportunity for students to bring together everything they have learned in their courses. (See "Appendix A. Choosing a Topic.") This report should be rigorous and analytical, not a simple descriptive paper. The following five areas are foundational to your paper's analysis:

- **Problem statement.** The problem statement must define a public policy issue that imposes substantial costs on society. The statement should be simple, and it should not include the solution as part of the problem. Although the problem statement can be narrow, it should not eliminate potential alternative policies. The problem statement is your paper's critical starting point: If it is wrong, then your entire analysis will be flawed.

- **Outcome definition.** The outcome definition must also be correct and relate to the problem statement. The outcome should be the goal of the program, and it must be measurable in physical, not monetary units—for, example, the number of graduates of a high school or college, not the number admitted or in attendance.

- **Calculation of cost-effectiveness.** This measure should be the dominant consideration in determining your final recommendation. If it is incorrect or missing, then your paper will—be of little value as a decision document in the political world.

- **Data from primary sources.** It is important to always use primary sources as opposed to secondary sources from a newspaper or a research organization. The most accurate data are generally from the federal government, as these data are based on a high standard for collection and are generally reconciled with other federal data. For example, Gross Domestic Product is measured by collecting data on both the product and income sides that are then reconciled, thereby enhancing their quality.

- **Reliance on data and metrics.** Use data and metrics throughout your paper. Whether your focus is on tons of carbon dioxide emissions or the number of vehicle-miles driven, provide substantial data and compare them with other data from other regions to provide perspective on the problem.

This guide discusses these five foundational issues in depth because they are what will make your analysis rigorous, which in turn will make your final paper valuable in the policy world. In addition, the guide provides context and information about other components of a quality capstone paper.

The Ivory Tower and the Mud Hut

Generally, to create a quality paper, you must have one foot in the ivory tower and one foot in the mud hut. By "ivory tower," I mean using the correct concept, collecting the best data and incorporating the best evidence from other studies. You must also pull together reliable historical data and use proven methodologies to make estimates and projections, particularly for outcomes and costs (and thus, cost-effectiveness measures). In other words, push the envelope to quantify the critical variables.

By "mud hut," I mean developing relationships with individuals who are deeply involved in the issue you are researching. (See "Appendix B. Creating a Mud Hut of Advisers.") These relationships are often with two types of individuals: academics and researchers currently working in your topic area and individuals involved in programs in your topic area. For example, if your topic is welfare reform, then you should not only talk to the deputy assistant secretary in your state government but the intake worker in the district office and an applicant for welfare. A quality report combines data-driven analysis and real-world information received from program participants and other issue experts.

The Client

Create your capstone paper for a real client, preferably for an office or agency in a city, state or the federal government. (See "Appendix B. Choosing and Working with a Client.") You could also do your report for a committee or member of a state legislature or Congress. Alternatively, develop a report for a nonprofit entity or local advocate. The lines between for-profit and nonprofit organizations are clearly shrinking, but for-profit organizations have different incentives and thus are not likely to make the best clients. Because capstones are generally for a public policy class at a college or university, it is better to consider clients without a conflict of interest with your school.

Working with a client presents a serious challenge because you will have to reconcile major components of the paper with the requirements of the public policy school (as advocated by your professor) and your client's desires. The result of this process is a real-world situation that provides a good learning experience. Throughout your working relationship with the client, you must maintain your objectivity, particularly regarding your final recommendation. It may be difficult to tell clients that they are not defining the problem correctly or that their preferred solution will not work long term, but you may also prevent them from making a serious error in judgment.

Special Emphasis

This guide also emphasizes several areas that other books on writing a capstone paper consider less important. First, I highlight program financing throughout the guide because different legislative committees make these funding decisions on different timelines from the enactment of program authorization. Financing decisions also face unique process and political obstacles at the federal government as Congress enacts many authorizations each year that never receive funding; therefore, the programs never become operational.

Second, this guide emphasizes making back-of-the-envelope estimates because there is rarely time to use the more sophisticated approaches found in the academic world.

Third, the guide discusses some of the nitty-gritty steps necessary to transform concepts into quantitative information for decision-makers.

Fourth, I detail policy levers other than amendments to existing laws or completely new laws. In today's highly partisan world, more elected executives are turning to issuing rules, regulations, executive orders and other types of guidance to avoid the legislative process. This book provides more information about the processes used to promulgate rules and regulations and when they may or may not be appropriate.

Finally, this guide places more emphasis on policy implementation because often this is where policy fails. Increasingly, these failures have contributed to the growing lack of trust among citizens in the United States. Policy implementation must be integrated into the early stages of policy development and funding. Similarly, the basis for the promulgation of rules and regulations and must be incorporated into the legislation. Actual implementation will take place after the legislation has been adopted, but success will depend on having the right team with the appropriate expertise, especially in technology. Success also requires necessary funding and staff members who do not oppose the newly enacted law.

Finally, a detailed implementation timeline—a working document that lists the milestones, activities, responsible parties and estimated time for individual task execution—is imperative. This document may also include costs, expected obstacles and objectives, contractors to be used and outside groups to be briefed. The timeline is a living document that is continuously vetted and revised during the implementation process.

Chapter 2
The Problem, the Outcome, and the Costs to Society

This chapter focuses on the first steps in your comprehensive analysis of a public policy issue. It starts by defining the problem, and then discusses the outcome, which should be consistent with the problem statement. Next, it outlines how you measure the costs of the problem to society. At this point, the costs-to-society measure does not have to be a comprehensive in-depth analysis; rather, it is more of a preliminary "ballpark" estimate before the full analysis. If the social costs to society are high, then the analysis should clearly proceed. If not, rethink whether in-depth analysis is needed. If the analysis goes forward, you can include a more in-depth discussion of costs in the context of cost-effectiveness measures later in the process.

The Problem Statement

The problem statement is a core definition, and it must be correct because it drives the entire analysis. This statement is essentially part of the rigorous framework required to make reliable recommendations. Start with a short, simple definition of a public policy problem.[1] Think in terms of a surplus or a deficit, or too much or too little. For example, "There are too many rent-burdened individuals living in Richmond, Virginia. 'Rent burdened' is generally defined as paying more than 30% of income on rent." Do not restrict the definition in any way or attempt to build a potential solution into the problem by saying, for example, "Because the city of Richmond does not subsidize rent, there are too many rent-burdened individuals living there."

Another appropriate problem statement—this time on health care—is, "Too many African Americans do not receive health care in Denver, Colorado." You do not want to say that they do not have health insurance. Rather, you want to state why they do not receive health care, whether due to lack of transportation, the inability to afford co-payments or a host of other reasons. You do not want to say, "Too many African Americans do not receive health care because health insurance is too expensive." Again, this statement is too restrictive because it implies that you are just looking at a narrow set of policy options, focused on affordability, versus addressing broader questions of access to care.

The elementary and secondary education arena offers several potential problem examples, such as "the drop-out

---

[1] Bardach, E., and Patashnik, E. M. (2015). *A practical guide for policy analysis: The eightfold path to more effective problem solving* (5th ed.). CQ Press.

rate in the Bridgeport, Connecticut, high school is too high" or "the number of fourth graders in Soldier's Elementary School in Plymouth, Massachusetts, who are not proficient in math, is too high." In higher education, the problem is generally that too few are graduating as opposed to simply having access to education. With such a problem statement, you will be able to compare different types of policies, some that focus on increasing access and others, such as mentoring, that focus on increasing the graduation rate. In the criminal justice area, a problem could be that "too few incarcerated individuals in Seattle have access to higher education classes."

In the environmental arena, a potential public policy problem could be that "the carbon dioxide emissions from the power plants in Dayton, Ohio, are too high" or "the amount of plastic waste that ends up in Lake Erie is too high."

The problem statement should be expressed in physical units, such as tons of carbon dioxide or the number of individuals living below the poverty line. All of the above statements are short sentences, with no adjectives to restrict them or to introduce potential solutions. This structure is important because it enables you to consider the maximum number of policies to resolve the issue. Here are five problem statements that need improvement.

Problem Statement 1

"The increased use of community supervision and the extraordinarily high incarceration rates for nonviolent offenses destabilizes families and communities and represents an economic threat to the Commonwealth of Virginia."

Two different concerns arise here. First, the statement essentially identifies several potential problems: high incarceration rates, destabilization of families and communities and an economic threat to the commonwealth. The outcome and costs of these problems are different and cannot be combined; therefore, rewrite the statement to focus on just one of the problems.

The second concern is that a potential cause—community supervision is built into the statement. This approach may focus the policy alternatives more on the causes. A better problem statement would be, "The number of families and communities in the commonwealth of Virginia that have nonviolent offenders is too high."

Problem Statement 2

"The current processes that Go-Virginia regions use to identify and address workforce-related barriers to business growth are neither streamlined nor standardized."

This is a process problem, not a public policy problem. A better statement that focuses on a potential policy problem could be, "Economic growth in the commonwealth of Virginia is too slow."

Problem Statement 3

"Only 27% of children in New York are reading proficiently by the end of fourth grade."

This is an observation, not a public policy problem. You could convert this sentence to a problem statement as follows: "By the end of fourth grade, too few students in New York are proficient in reading."

Problem Statement 4

"The perceived and experienced difficulties of using the public transit system pose a significant challenge for take-up by the public."

This one is somewhat vague and has an awkward restriction of perceived and experienced difficulties. A better statement would be, "Ridership on public transit is too low."

Problem Statement 5

"Maryland has not fostered an environment conducive to returning service members and fails to attract more service members on an annual basis."

This statement is flawed because the issue is not a public policy problem. It is important to focus on an outcome. For example, "Too many returning service members to the state of Maryland are living in poverty" or "Too many returning service members are finding it difficult to transition to civilian jobs."

After you have developed the problem statement, provide some perspective on its significance. First, calculate the significance over time. Answer the question: Is the situation getting worse? And, if it is, how quickly is the situation deteriorating? Second, compare the significance to similar geographic regions. For example, if the geographic region is a large city, compare that city with other large cities. If the geographic region is a state, compare it with adjoining states, perhaps states similar in terms of Gross Domestic Product per person. If the geographic region is the United States, compare it with other Organization for Economic Cooperation and Development countries. These comparisons should be for both the most recent year and over a five- to 10-year period.

Outcome Vs. Output

The next most important task is to define the outcome of a specific program. It differs from the output, which is merely a measure of what has been produced from a program. Outputs do not address the value or impact of the service or program on the client. In contrast, the outcome includes a level of performance or achievement. In the example of a job training program, the output of the program could be the number of individuals enrolled or the number who graduate; the outcome is the number of enrolled individuals who both graduate and get a job. You are interested in maximizing the number who receive a job, not just the ones who graduate from the program.

In a high school education program, enrollment is an output, but the number of students who graduate is an outcome. Here, you want to minimize the number who drop out. In general, an outcome is a physical measure, such as the number of individuals who receive health care or tons of carbon dioxide or the number of homeless people. The outcome is not generally a value number, that uses dollars as the measure. The outcome is critical because it is part of the calculation of cost-effectiveness. and must be consistent with your problem statement.

It is possible to create a weighted outcome. For example, states are now moving away from using an output measure such as enrollment to allocate state funds to state universities and colleges. Instead, many are moving to graduation rates, which is more an outcome measure, because they create an incentive for universities and colleges to help students graduate by assisting them in several ways including financially. Given that states want to reduce inequality, there is also interest in increasing the number of graduates who are first-generation college attendees, from low-income populations and are people of color. Therefore, they may weight these graduates more heavily than others to create a larger incentive for universities and colleges to help these students graduate.

The Costs to Society

With the problem statement and outcome specified, your next task is to determine the costs that the identified problem imposes on society—a back-of-the-envelope calculation that helps you determine whether you should proceed with a comprehensive analysis. If the social costs are insignificant, then you may not want to proceed. In contrast, if the costs are significant, then a comprehensive analysis is in order.

The first step in quantifying the cost to society is to specify the geographic area of interest. The area could be the United States, an individual state, a city or another area.

Ideally, the geographic area should coincide with the jurisdiction of a government for which you evaluate alternative policies later in the analysis. Other governments can potentially affect the geographic region, but you can hold those governments constant in the analysis.

In calculating the costs to society, generate estimates for three different types of costs. First are the direct (i.e., out-of-pocket) costs that society pays to address the problem. Second are the economic (i.e., opportunity) costs, usually lost wages or economic output from the inability to work or from early death. Third are the costs stemming from externalities, such as degradation of the environment.

Direct Costs

To calculate direct costs, estimate both the number of people and the cost per person affected in the designated geographic region. For example, assume that the problem statement is, 'There are too many individuals in the commonwealth of Virginia who do not have access to health care. Essentially, most of these individuals are uninsured or underinsured. Let's assume that 100,000 people fall into this category who do not receive primary care, such as screening for diabetes or high blood pressure. Because of the lack of primary care, these people may end up in the emergency room (ER) of the local hospital—a high-cost impact. Assume that this cost is $800 per ER visit, and 6,000 of these 100,000 individuals had one ER visit in the year for a total cost of $4,800,000. These direct costs are observable and will be paid by the individual; a government program, such as Medicaid; or an uncompensated care fund that all other patients pay'.

At 55 or 65 years of age, an individual may have a stroke and become partially disabled, requiring a stay in a rehabilitation facility. The average stay in such a facility was 21 days at a daily rate of $1,200 and 600 individuals required such care. Thus, the total cost for this care was $15,120,000. These costs are eventually paid by some entity—Medicare or Medicaid, the state or local government, a private insurance company or other patients who pay for uncompensated care. The point is that society pays. This translates into a total direct cost of $19.920,000 for the 100,000 people who lacked insurance or lacked the ability to pay the co-pay for primary care screening in Virginia.

Economic Costs

Economic costs are those that society bears but does not pay directly. In the previous example, these costs would include the value of time lost from work because of emergency treatments, time in a rehabilitation facility or disability or early death. Assume that the 100,000 uninsured and underinsured people were not able to work, on average, 50 hours per year and that their average salary was $5 per hour, which would equal $250,000,000 in lost wages or alternatively in reductions in National Income or Gross National Product (GNP).[2]

---

[2] Refer to the U.S. Office of Management and Budget cost of a life, which is often used in this type of analysis.

Externalities

Externalities are essentially costs or benefits—side-effects or consequences of an activity—that are not reflected in the price of a good or service. Economists define these factors as costs or benefits not reflected in prices of consumer transactions or in the production of goods or services. When bees pollinate vegetables or fruits in the production of honey, this work would be considered a benefit over and above the value of the honey. In contrast, carbon dioxide emissions and climate change are important examples of externalities that impose substantial costs on society in the production of electricity. Plastic bottles ending up in the oceans are an example of a cost in the consumption of soda. The costs of these externalities are becoming a much greater percentage of the total costs to society given the density of our population and consumer behaviors.

In the health care example above, the externalities are minor, but an example would be to calculate the number of miles patient's drive to the hospital for emergency care, the level of carbon dioxide emissions per mile, and then the cost in terms of negative health and lifestyle impacts per ton of carbon. If you assume 6,000 trips to the hospital at an average of 10 miles per trip and emissions of five tons per 5,000 miles at a cost to health and lifestyle of $50 per ton of carbon, the total cost is $600. So, in summary the total cost to society is $19.920,000 in direct costs, $250,000,000 in productivity or opportunity costs and $600 for externalities, for a total cost to society of $44,269,920,600.

This analysis shows how to calculate the total social costs to society. It is a back-of-the-envelope approach to determine whether the costs are high enough to proceed with a full-blown analysis of the public policy problem. If high-quality estimates are available for the region from other analysts, use them. Most often, however, you will need to tailor the estimates to the specific geography of interest based on partial estimates by others. The literature is robust with respect to the three types of costs, which can generally be found in peer-reviewed journals. If it is not possible to generate a point estimate, use ranges.

Chapter 3
Setting the Stage

The early sections of your capstone report must set the stage so that your readers will be able to understand the analysis and recommendation that follow. Some students conduct an in-depth literature review and insert their findings into the paper; others prefer to divide the literature into topics rather than including everything under the heading of "Literature Review." Whichever way you approach it, the literature review is a critical part of your capstone report. The review is also a continuous process, and you will continue to fill in gaps missed in the initial review. This chapter not only summarizes how to do a literature review but discusses the key issues that need to addressed in setting the stage.

The Literature Review

A literature review involves searching and pulling together all the relevant information from books, journal articles and other sources on a specific topic. The findings from the review provide background and context on the issue and help you determine gaps in knowledge. The review should also include the methodologies used to develop estimates relevant to the policy issue you are researching. The goal is not just to find the information but, more importantly, to evaluate and summarize it. It is important that you be highly organized in performing the literature search; otherwise, you will lose valuable time and risk becoming frustrated and overwhelmed. The search must also be comprehensive and accurate, so be prepared to invest substantial time. Resources are available to help you organize your literature search.[3,4] The steps may differ somewhat, but here are five I recommend:

1. Determine the question and key words.
2. Search for relevant literature.
3. Evaluate the quality of the literature found.
4. Outline the structure of the review.
5. Write the literature review.

Step 1. Determine the Question and Key Words

Start by developing a well-defined policy question, one that is focused but not too narrow and complex enough to allow for substantial research. For example, the question

---

[3] McCombes, S. (2022, March 16). What is a literature review: Step-by-step guide and examples. *Scribbr.*
https://www.scribbr.com/dissertation/literature-review/

[4] Sriram, R. (2018, May 1). How to do an effective literature search in 5 steps. *Kolabtree Blog.*
https://www.kolabtree.com/blog/how-to-do-an-effective-literature-search-in-5-steps/

could be, "Why are so many low-income Americans without health care?" It may even be helpful to develop a few additional questions, such as, "Why are so few low-income Americans eligible for Medicaid?" and "Why do so many Americans lack access to doctors and hospitals?"

From these questions, you can develop the key words to search. Start with the core words, then include any synonym or related term. Include different spellings, variants and tenses. Before starting the search, read several articles from various sources to get a sense of key words. Determining the right key words helps minimize gaps in the search.

Step 2. Search for Relevant Literature

The search should be comprehensive and include a variety of sources. There are essentially two types of databases: multidisciplinary databases, which are broad, and databases that focus on a discipline (e.g., economics). Start your search with books and articles from peer-reviewed journals, but do not ignore nonobvious sources, such as conference proceedings, ongoing research at universities, online discussion forums or databases of high-quality material, and doctoral dissertations. Always get guidance from university librarians, who are both highly qualified and willing to help.

Useful general databases include Google Scholar, JSTOR and EBSCO. Issue-specific databases include Education Resources Information Center, which has 1.5 million records of education research; EconLit for economics literature; and Project MUSE for humanities and social sciences. Read the abstract to see if the article is relevant to your question. If it is, check the article's "References" section to find other relevant sources. As you read the articles, take notes that you can later incorporate into the text of the literature review. It is critical that you keep track of all sources by using citations; it may even make sense to compile an annotated bibliography, with a paragraph summary of key articles.

Step 3. Evaluate the Quality of the Literature Found

Now that you have all the information, determine which sources are the most reliable and credible. For articles, prioritize those in peer-reviewed journals. For example, the journal Health Affairs is peer reviewed, but its accompanying blog is not: Generally, the higher-quality research is in the journal. It is also important to look at authors' credentials and whether the authors reference key information. When the article was published is also important. Every discipline has some classic articles, but dated articles may be less reliable because the structure of programs, demographic changes or technology may render the conclusions obsolete.

Make sure that the sources you rely on are credible; in particular, read any landmark studies and theories, particularly new ones that may be in opposition to the traditional theory. For example, if your focus is on federal deficits and the growing U.S debt, be sure to read about modern monetary theory, which questions traditional theories on government debt and revenues. You should also include new and innovative ideas. Finally, it helps to indicate where articles are reinforcing other articles in conclusions, theories or methodology and where they conflict.

Step 4. Outline the Structure of the Review

How you organize the literature review depends to some extent on the issue you are researching and your preferences. Consider the following options:

- **Chronologically.** This approach may be the easiest, but it makes sense only if you can point out turning points and events that changed a trend.
- **By theme.** For example, if the issue is lack of health care for low-income individuals, themes include federal policy changes, cultural attitudes, economic profiles and legal status.
- **Methodology.** When methodology is the organizing principal, it should be possible to distinguish qualitative from quantitative analysis or ex post facto from ex ante facto analysis.
- **Empirical versus theoretical.** It may be possible to differentiate purely empirical research from literature that depends on an underlying theoretical foundation. You could even organize the empirical studies around several alternative theories.

Step 5. Write the Literature Review

If your literature review will stand alone, it should start with an introduction that talks about the public policy issue you are researching to provide focus and explain the purpose of the review. The body of the report is not just a summary but an analysis, synthesis and critical evaluation of the information. Finally, a conclusion highlights the major take-aways. If you plan to integrate the literature review into the report, determine where in the report the review findings fit based on the report outline, then write the sections for integration later.

Metrics and Data

To strengthen the discussions in the report, back up critical points with appropriate statistics and data. Numeric data can be particularly persuasive and sharpen key points.[5] There are essentially two types of data: (1) data that have already been collected and published, generally by a federal agency, and (2) data that you collect. The latter data can include your observations, surveys or interviews that you conduct or information you record in a lab or in the field. You can use either informal information or more formal data that meet certain statistical standards, for sample size and confidence levels. That said, you should not rely so heavily on statistics that you lose your ability to emphasize key points. Even for data available from a federal agency, quality is important, and so check on how the data were collected and whether the data are a sample (and if so, what was the sample size) or a full census.

---

[5] Teaching and Learning, Ohio State University Libraries. (n.d.). Data as sources. In *Choosing and using sources: A guide to academic research.* Pressbooks. https://ohiostate.pressbooks.pub/choosingsources/chapter/data-as-sources

Use numeric data for key points, but try to provide maximum information in the minimum number of words.[6] For example, actual numbers for two years and the rate of growth in between is an example of maximum information. It is also critical that you be specific about the concept used. For example, postsecondary graduation rates can be defined over four or six years. Income can be defined on a pre- or post-tax basis with or without transfer payments. Similarly, several measures for unemployment are available. The bottom line is that you must define the concept and use the correct data series. It is also important to use original sources for all data. Generally, your sources will be federal agencies, such as the U.S. Census Bureau or the Bureau of Labor Statistics.

At times, you may need to include tables, charts or graphs in your report. As with data, do not overuse these graphics. Each graphic needs a number; a title at the top; and, where appropriate, a label on each axis. Include the source of the element beneath it. Finally, refer to the graphic in the preceding narrative, and indicate the important take-away from it.

Where no quantitative data are available, lean on qualitative information, which is defined as data that approximates and characterizes concepts. These data are non-numerical but can be observed and recorded. Collection methods include one-on-one interviews, focus groups, record keeping, process of observation and the

---

[6] QuestionPro. (n.d.). *Qualitative data—definition, types, analysis and examples.* Retrieved April 9, 2022, from https://www.questionpro.com/blog/qualitative-data/

inductive approach. Some argue that qualitative data are helpful in providing more in-depth analysis because they get into the thought process and explain why a decision was made. Gathering qualitative data can be time-consuming, however, and these data may not be easy to generalize and may depend on the skill of the questioner. Depending on the public policy problem you are researching and the availability of numeric data, you should use both quantitative and qualitative measures.

A Perspective on the Problem

It is critical that you provide substantial perspective on the problem so that your readers have a good sense of the seriousness. If the problem has to do with dropout rates for a particular high school in Chicago, Illinois, for example, then it is important to provide data for the preceding 10 years to determine whether the problem has become more serious over time. It is also important to include how the data compare with other schools in Chicago; the state average; and the average for other schools in the state that have similar demographics, including employment, education, income and marriage rates.

You may also want to make comparisons with a couple of schools in other cities in other states that have similar demographics. Choose cities in adjoining states so that the schools are in the same region. Similar comments can be made regarding state and national comparisons. For example, the United States should be compared with other Western countries using Organization for Economic

Cooperation and Development data because these countries have similar government structures and cultures.

The Causes of the Problem

Consider in the context discussion the major causes of the problem or the contributing factors. This information may be easy to develop if there is a clear consensus; other times, views may be conflicting. Either way, the potential causes are important for providing direction with respect to determining the alternative policies you will include in your analysis. Here is a case in point: The causes of the high cost of health care are shown in Figure 1. When looking at options for building cost control into the Patient Protection and Affordable Care Act (ACA), several causes stood out. First, administrative costs were high; second, the fee-for-service payment system increased the frequency of the number of tests and procedures; and third, the system was fragmented and uncoordinated. These findings led Congress to create a new office in the U.S. Department of Health and Human Services (HHS) to focus on innovations in health care. This legislation eventually led to the development of accountable care organizations (ACOs), a new delivery system model that included incentives to reduce costs and increase quality.[7] Further, the legislation

---

[7] HHS defines "fully integrated ACOs" as groups of doctors, hospitals and other health care providers who come together voluntarily to provide coordinated, high-quality care to their Medicare patients. The goal of coordinated care is to ensure that patients get the right care at the right time while avoiding

included significant funds for HHS to set up a major demonstration program to get this new model fully operational and part of the U.S. health care system. Medicare is now in the process of changing their reimbursement system to advantage ACOs relative to fee-for-service providers.

Essentially, HHS created and demonstrated a new delivery system entity that would hopefully reduce the major drivers of high health costs in Figure 1, particularly numbers 3, 5 and 6. The demonstrations are continuing as we now close to 500 ACOs operating in the United States. The results to date are mixed but the point is new policies may have to be developed by asking the question: How might we get rid of several major causes of the problem?

---

unnecessary duplication of services and preventing medical errors. When an ACO succeeds in delivering high-quality care and spending health care dollars more wisely, the ACO shares in the savings it achieves for the Medicare program.

Comparison of cost for common procedures											
	Argentina	Spain	France	Canada	Germany	Chile	Australia	Switzerland	US-Low	U-S Average	US-High
Normal delivery (Physician fee)	163	329	449	536	226	890	1837	NA	2397	3096	5407
Normal delivery (Facility and fee)	1188	2765	3541	3195	2157	2992	6846	4039	7262	9775	16653
C-Section (Physician fee)	193	428	938	606	402	1084	2118	NA	2688	3676	6593
C-Section (Fee and Facility)	1541	3097	6441	5980	3441	3778	10566	5186	10545	15041	26305
Cataract (Physician fee)	157	420	426	699	609	1048	1311	NA	651	922	1839
Cataract (Fee and Facility)	564	1867	1938	2358	2514	2829	3591	2566	2418	3738	8143
Appendectomy (Physician fee)	148	231	776	408	258	724	782	NA	674	1001	2044
Appendectomy (Fee and Facility)	953	2245	4463	5606	3093	4221	5467	4782	8156	13851	29426
Hp Replacement (Physician fee)	461	1088	1288	697	644	1992	2883	NA	1983	2888	5196
Hp Replacement (Fee and Facility)	3365	7931	10937	16945	11418	13409	27810	9574	25061	40364	87987
Routine office visit (Physician fee)	10	11	30	30	40	38	NA	64	68	95	176
CT Scan (Abdomen)	103	118	183	124	354	234	NA	437	243	630	1737
MRI	118	230	363	NA	599	502	NA	928	522	1121	2871

Figure 1. The Drivers of High Health Care Costs in the United States

1. Physician, facility and drug costs are high.
2. Americans use a higher proportion of expensive medicine.
3. Care is fragmented and uncoordinated.
4. Consumers with health insurance do not weigh costs when making care decisions.
5. The traditional fee-for-service payment system contributes to frequency of use and high cost.
6. Administrative expenditures are high.
7. Americans often make unhealthy lifestyle choices.
8. End-of-life care is expensive.
9. Provider consolidation in some regions pushes prices higher.

Source: State Health Care Cost Containment Commission. (2014, January 19). *Cracking the code on health care costs.* The Miller Center, University of Virginia. https://millercenter.org/issues-policy/us-domestic-policy/the-state-health-care-cost-containment-commission

The Jurisdiction of Different Levels of Government

The level of government on which you are focusing your analysis requires a deep dive in terms of the applicable laws, rules and regulations as well as the offices and agencies involved. Any alternative policies you will discuss later needs to have a full discussion of existing policy at this point, as well. For example, if you are proposing amending a particular law as an alternative policy, fully discuss that law in the government section. Similarly, if an alternative policy is to promulgate a different rule or amend a regulation, then fully discuss the existing rules here. In addition, include a full discussion of the agency that has jurisdiction over the policy. In some areas such as electricity regulation, commissions have substantial decision-making authority. In such a case, discuss the laws that established the commission, how the commission members were appointed and the scope of the commission's jurisdiction. Given that all three levels of government have some impact on your problem it is important to include these in your discussion as well but be clear these policies will be frozen in your analysis.

Technology

A critical link exists between technological change and the various policy options. Generally, it is assumed that the historical rate of technological change will continue at the same rate into the future. Today, however, technological change is rapid, and new, disruptive technologies are being developed every year. Examples abound: electric vehicles, cloud computing, 3D printing, robotics, next-generation storage, mobile internet and artificial intelligence. But what if there is a high probability of a technological breakthrough, a game changer in terms of enhancing quality or productivity or reducing costs?

A case in point could be solar energy with enhanced battery storage. Such a technology would dramatically decrease electricity costs per kilowatt-hour. A house powered by solar energy could be completely off the electricity grid or remain connected but sell to the grid. To date, 17 states have passed laws that allow net energy metering, often called "aggregated" or "net distributed energy." In those states, a school, a business or house can install solar energy, sell any surplus to the utility at a retail rate, and receive a credit toward their own electricity bill. This technology is a game changer because the utility may no longer have to expand capacity, which often costs billions of dollars. It could also change how the state regulates that utility.

There are several ways to discuss technology change. First, a higher rate of change could be incorporated into one or two of the policy options that reflect the breakthrough. The new rate should reflect a consensus of experts. The second way is to assume that technological change will be consistent with the historical rate in the analysis, but then discuss it in a technology section, including how it will affect the results. Third and perhaps best, depending on the assumed rate of change, there could be a hybrid solution, where some technological change is incorporated into one or two relevant options while still addressing the issue elsewhere in a technology section.

Best Practices

One of the most important sections of setting the stage is the evidence or best practice information discussion that you use later to project your outcomes for your cost-effectiveness measures. Specifically, use studies that reflect what happened with respect to outcomes in other cities, states or school districts when they made similar policies changes. Ex post facto examples are the best type of information, but such examples are often not available; thus, you may have to use ex ante facto studies. Of primary interest here is the percentage change in outcomes relative to current policy at specific times after the policy changes were implemented.

The quality of the estimates is critical. Ex post facto experience is more important than ex ante facto studies, and peer-reviewed ex ante facto studies are generally more reliable than those that are not reviewed. It is also true that even the best studies may provide information for only two points on the projection time horizon, which is often 10 years into the future. Thus, you must assume a trajectory based on only those two points plus informed judgement.

Remember that state and local governments often beg, borrow and steal best policies from each other when those policies are found to be effective. The saying most often heard from state policy staff is, "We do not have to reinvent the wheel." State or local governments tend to make incremental policy adjustments to improve on the work of other state or local governments.

This research is best done by a disinterested third party who is involved in the evaluation when a new program is initiated. For example, assume that the problem is high dropout rates in a particular high school. Then, assume that the principal adopts a new program that requires all teachers to make recommendations on students at risk of dropping out. Then, two new teachers are hired who have specialized training to assist these high-risk students. The principal then hires a professor from the local college to create a tracking system on dropouts as part of the evaluation.

A major problem is that little of the information collected by state and local governments is published. Therefore, you must be able to tap into existing networks of information. For states, the National Governors Association, the Council of State Governments and the National Conference of State Legislatures all collect this information and may make it available to researchers, even in unpublished form. In addition, other organizations that represent state executives or agencies, such as the National Association of State Budget Officers or the National Association of Medicaid Directors, maintain valuable data. Similar associations exist for local governments, such as the United States Conference of Mayors, the National League of Cities and the National Association of Counties, which collect similar types of information. Often, no information is publicly available, but individuals who work for these organizations are often aware of state or local governments that have changed policies. You can gather much of this information by interviewing individuals currently administering the state or local programs.

Best practice information is seldom similar to the program under consideration. Therefore, you must be prepared to use your imagination and push the envelope in gathering information. Sometimes, the information will have to come from other countries or even cities in other countries. Other times, the only available information may come from a similar program. For example, say that you are interested in the impact of a work requirement on the number of individuals enrolled in a state Medicaid program.

Unfortunately, the only data that may be available is for a work requirement for the Supplemental Nutrition Assistance Program in a different state. Responsiveness to a work requirement may be similar, however, because similar populations are eligible for both programs.

Quality, Proficiency, and Other Factors

For most public policy issues, other unique factors may be key and should be discussed as part of setting the stage. For example, a major problem in the health care arena is the cost of care, which has a huge impact not only on access to care but on federal and state budgets. It is difficult to talk about the cost of health care, however, without also discussing quality because policies to reduce costs may have negative impacts on quality of care. This dichotomy was seen years ago when managed care was thought to be effective in reducing costs. Instead, it just reduced access to care. Therefore, it is critical to discuss all the metrics used to measure quality—metrics for health insurance companies, for nursing homes, for ACOs and for other providers. Quality may also have to be one criterion in the final analysis if the problem statement focuses on costs.

A similar situation arises for elementary and secondary education. For example, if the problem is one of high dropout rates in secondary schools, then proficiency measures must be discussed while setting the stage, to guard against lowering standards to reduce dropouts. Quality and proficiency are just two such examples but there are potentially many more depending on the problem statement.

50

Chapter 4
Alternative Policies

In choosing policy alternatives, it is important to go broad: Start with four or five policies in addition to the status quo. In this way, you can jettison one or possibly two policies as you gather more information. The final analysis should include a minimum of three alternatives in addition to the status quo to have a reliable, comprehensive approach. It is important to include alternatives—some incremental and some bold. Think outside the box, and develop at least one nontraditional approach. To the extent that market approaches would work, give them a high priority because they are often more sustainable at minimum cost. Throughout the development of alternative policies, remember that there is a difference between authorizing a program and funding it. Therefore, for many policies, both should be included.

A Caution on the Need for New Policies

A bias in the public policy arena is that there is always a need for a new policy. Sometimes, the better approach is to sunset ineffective programs, rules and regulations. Stop to consider the following potential risks of a new policy:

- **Many bad policies have been adopted.** Bad policies are adopted because of unintended consequences or because the policy was either misconceived or badly implemented. Some bad policies are enacted after a crisis, such as a policy enacted after a warehouse fire that imposes substantial costs on an industry by mandating installation of sprinklers, the cost of which is out of proportion to the costs of a fire.
- **The current policy does not impose substantial costs on society.** As indicated in Chapter 2, it is important to determine whether the current policy imposes substantial costs on society. Too often, analysts commit to a new policy before completing an objective analysis.
- **Public support is limited for new programs and regulations.** The United States and individual states have reached a level of maturity regarding laws and regulations. Many of these laws and regulations are appropriate, but the cumulative impact has reduced the freedom of citizens and businesses; thus, public support for new policies is

limited. All three levels of government should constantly review existing laws, rules and regulations and repeal those that are no longer effective. Be aware that the bar for new policies is higher now than it was 30 years ago because of limited public support.

- **Most government policies interfere with the market and thus create inefficiencies.** Whether it is a new program, rule or regulation, most government actions interfere with the free market and thus lower efficiency. Often, public policy is a tradeoff between efficiency and equity. The cost of lower efficiency is that you likely also lower national output, income, real wages and the standard of living of all Americans. Such policies may be appropriate to protect consumers or provide transparency, but they are not without costs.

- **The larger the public sector, the lower national productivity.** It is generally assumed that government has zero productivity. In contrast, the private sector has averaged 2.2% change in productivity over the 2008–18 period.[8] This productivity change is the source of all increases in real wages and real income in the United States. Therefore, remember that increasing the size of government will likely reduce the rate of increase in real income. This effect can be seen in the international arena, where many European countries witness lower growth

---

[8] U.S. Bureau of Labor Statistics. (2021, April 21). The monthly labor report.

than the United States. Clearly, a contributing factor is that the government sector is a much larger share of national income in these countries.

Any one of these factors should make you pause, but together, they raise the bar in terms of adopting new policies. Instead, consider sunsetting existing laws, programs, rules and regulations that may impose costs but offer no benefits to society.

Define the Status Quo

It is important to have a clearly defined status quo or baseline, a point at which all laws, regulations and funding levels are assumed to be frozen (e.g., Oct. 1, 2020). This baseline would apply to all three levels of government. One challenge is what you assume for an authorization that sunsets during the time period of your analysis. In general, if a program has witnessed several previous reauthorizations, then it is generally assumed that it will be renewed again. For those laws that will come up for their first reauthorization during your designated time frame, it is best to make an explicit assumption regarding reauthorization.

There are also times when your analysis depends on another level of government enacting a major initiative. For example, in evaluating several policies designed to help inmates in a state prison achieve a four-year college degree, inmates' eligibility for Pell grants was a game changer. The eligibility was eliminated in 2009 but restored in 2021. If you were writing a capstone paper on this issue in 2020, then it would have been fine to assume that Pell grant eligibility would be reauthorized in 2021 in your status quo. It is often safe to assume that Congress will pass some large legislative initiative that is critical for the state analysis.

Authorization and Funding

It is critical that you distinguish the actual policy, which is often referred to as the "authorization," from the funding it requires. At both the state and federal levels, many authorizations of new programs are enacted each year but never funded. Therefore, when choosing a policy, you must specify the funding mechanism in addition to the authorization.

Most new programs will require funding to assist the target population as well as to cover the staff and other costs to administer the program. Even the adoption of new rules and regulations may require some oversight or enforcement, which in turn requires staffing and funding. Most funding is provided by an appropriations committee at the federal level or an appropriations or finance committee at the state level. These committees are separate from the committees that authorize the new programs.

That said, programs at the federal level that provide benefits directly to individuals such as Social Security, the Supplemental Nutrition Assistance Program or Medicare are entitlements, which means that the authorization and funding are combined in one bill or law. Essentially, the law sets forth eligibility for benefits; then, all who qualify automatically receive those benefits. Medicaid is another entitlement at both the federal and state levels. The advantage of an entitlement is that the benefits are guaranteed and, in general, the appropriations committee has no role. The disadvantage is that it is difficult to control entitlement spending over time.

At the federal level, there are also many mandatory programs, such as farm price supports, where the spending is automatic and bypasses appropriations committees. At times, it may be important to create a trust fund or to dedicate a revenue stream to a new program. For example, states often dedicate entrance fees to state parks to a fund that pays for maintaining and renovating those parks. Depending on the state, it may be possible to create and dedicate the fee and authorize spending in one bill. If it is a new tax to fund a new program, then it is likely that the tax must be authorized by a separate finance committee. At the federal level, this would be the Ways and Means Committee in the House of Representatives and the Finance Committee in the Senate.

An example of a trust fund at the federal level is the Highway Trust Fund, which receives federal gasoline tax revenues. Dedicated revenues for programs or trust funds have the advantage of sustaining the program, but they create huge inefficiencies in that revenues may not equal the required funding. Revenues generally fall short or create huge surpluses. The bottom line is that you must make two decisions for each policy—the authorization and the funding—and include both in the description of the policy. This also means that any discussion of political feasibility, equity or the ability to implement the program must include both the authorization and the funding.

Phasing in Large Initiatives

In the past, tax bills have at times phased in the effective date. For example, the 1969 Tax Reform Act phased in the personal exemption from $600 to $700. Similarly, the penalty for not having health insurance in the Patient Protection and Affordable Care Act (ACA) in 2010 was phased in. Starting in 2014, the maximum family penalty amount was $285. This amount increased to $975 in 2015, and then to $2,085 in 2016. This approach gave citizens time to purchase health care. The provision was repealed in 2018. A similar example was how the COVID-19 vaccines were phased in by state, starting with the highest-risk individuals, older Americans and health care workers.

In the National Federation of Independent Business v. Sebelius decision, the U.S. Supreme Court declared that the mandated Medicaid expansion was unconstitutional. This decision allowed states to decide whether they wanted to act on the new system, which made everyone below 138% of poverty eligible. Given that this expansion was potentially huge, many states looked for ways to phase it in. Some states considered a phase-in by income class (e.g., in the first six months, everyone below 100% of poverty would become eligible; in the next six months, those up to 120% of poverty would be eligible; then in the third six months, those up to 148% of poverty would be eligible). Other states considered a phase-in by region. In the final analysis, legal and political obstacles arose, so no state phased in the expansion.

Nevertheless, a phased implementation generally has three major advantages. First, it gives the individual recipient of the benefit time to gather additional information and determine eligibility. Second, implementation of every policy runs into unanticipated problems. Administrators can use this delay to fix the problems before going to the next stage. Third, a smooth implementation enhances the public's trust in government.

The Role of Technology

Generally, all the analysis you do for your capstone paper will be static. Static analysis assumes that the rate of technological change in the past will continue into the future. Alternatively, it could mean that change will be certain, regular, constant and thus predictable. Across the board, however, more and more disruptive technologies are becoming available. We see these technologies in the expansion of the cloud, robotics, battery storage, the metaverse, artificial intelligence, self-driving vehicles, quantum computing and blockchain, to name just a few. These new technologies have the potential to dramatically reduce the costs of some products or can significantly increase the output per unit of input (i.e., productivity) for some products. Further, they have the capacity to transform entire industries. This rate of change means that you should research any technology involved and make explicit assumptions for both the base case and all the alternative policies, particularly if you expect the rate to be different in the future.

Describe Each Alternative

You will need to estimate the total cost of each alternative you identify in your paper. To that end, provide as much detail as possible at this early stage. Indicate whether the policy requires new legislation or can be done administratively through rules or regulations. If the latter, then which secretary of a given agency has jurisdiction over the issue? If it requires new legislation, which existing law must be amended? If you are proposing stand-alone legislation, clearly indicate as much. If you are proposing a rule change, what is the underlying regulation? For tax changes, you must give the exact change—for example, increasing the state sales tax from 4.75% to 4.90% of the retail value. Provide information about both the authorization level and the appropriation level for any new programs.

Choose Alternative Policies

Choosing appropriate policies is at the heart of your analysis because the bar to adoption or enactment of any policy today is high. First, identify any options that improve the operation of the market. These alternatives are often superior to interfering with the market because they tend to create inefficiencies. Also, market approaches are easier to sustain over the long term.

Second, avoid limiting the choices to the traditional approaches. Early on, it is critical to think outside the box and look for nontraditional approaches. After that, you may want to consider incremental approaches that represent limited interventions, such as collecting and sharing new information with the public or requiring an industry to place certain information in the public domain to increase transparency. They could also include public awareness campaigns, such as those during 2020 and 2021 regarding vaccinations against COVID-19. From there, consider several moderately intrusive approaches, such as creating and enforcing new standards or modifying rules or regulations. Finally, it may be appropriate to choose more intrusive or bolder approaches, such as those that involve new taxes or programs.

Make the Market Work

Sometimes, the public policy problem is that a market is not working. If a policy can be adopted that encourages or creates a rational market, then you should include it as an alternative option. One success of the ACA is that it assisted in making the individual or small-group health care market work. Most individuals in the United States receive their care either through the two government-run programs (Medicare and Medicaid) or through the so-called Employee Retirement Income Security Act (ERISA) firms, which are large corporations that provide employer-paid insurance to their employees. Before enactment of the ACA, other individuals had to purchase their health care through the individual and small-group market, where insurance firms rated an individual's risk based on health status and age. The result was that premiums were substantially higher than that of the ERISA firms—for some individuals, so high that they had to go without insurance. So, those with the poorest health who needed insurance the most were not insurable. In 2008, this individual or small group market population may have included as many as 8 million people. The ACA prohibited insurance companies from risk-rating individuals, and it created health care exchanges or marketplaces in each state through which consumers could buy and insurance companies could sell insurance. In 2022, almost 14 million individuals purchased their health insurance through the exchanges. These exchanges are also where the federal government subsidies individuals whose incomes are below 400%of poverty but are not eligible for Medicaid. In 2021, an additional 30 insurance companies decided to sell policies in 20 states, and 61 companies have expanded their footprint in the states. Now, five health insurance companies on average sell insurance in each state.[9] The state or federal rules require companies to provide premium, deductibles and co-pay information consistently so that consumers can compare costs. Currently, orderly and robust markets exist in each state.

---

[9] McDermott, D., and Cox, C. (2020, November 23). Insurer participation on the ACA marketplaces, 2014–2021 [Tweet]. Twitter.

Think Outside the Box

Too often, students restrict their alternatives to traditional policies when a nontraditional approach may be best. Particularly in the early phase of policy exploration, select at least one nontraditional approach.

Take policies to reduce the number of residents of Richmond who are rent burdened—as in, paying more than 30% of their income on rent. Students typically look at providing subsidies to low-income individuals through vouchers or requiring builders to build a certain percentage of their homes for low-income individuals. These options may work to lower the cost of housing but so might increasing individuals' income. You could propose boosting incomes by creating a training program in partnership with the private sector. You could also suggest an increase in the city's minimum wage. One or more of these strategies that increase income as opposed to lowering the cost of housing may well be the most cost-effective solutions for alleviating the rent burden for the most significant number of families.

Incremental Changes

After looking at market and nontraditional approaches, consider some small, incremental policy alternatives. These policies are often effective and will minimize the citizen backlash. In addition, they are often more easily adopted and implemented. If they fall short, they can be strengthened over time. Examples of incremental changes include providing information, educating the public and setting a new standard.

Providing Information

An important role of government is to provide objective, unbiased and transparent information to citizens directly or mandate that a particular industry do it so the public can make educated decisions. The Food and Drug Administration requires food labeling that displays fat content, sodium levels and other nutritional information. Many of these mandates are opposed by specific industries, but they often have broad public support and are far less intrusive than other approaches. Transparency is one of the best policy arrows in the quiver of public leaders.

State and local governments are often also required to publish proposed budget information by agency so that the public knows where tax revenues are spent. These governments may also be required to publish performance measures so that the public knows the cost for each call for an ambulance or each rental subsidy. This information may need to be posted online for ease of access. Citizens can then compare this information over time and with other jurisdictions.

Educating the Public

Government-initiated public health and education campaigns, especially those based on high-quality research, are often extremely effective in bringing information to citizens. The campaigns can run through a combination of print and digital media. The federal government, states and localities have launched campaigns on issues such as educating citizens about the hazards of smoking, the benefits of taking public transit, where to receive a vaccine against COVID-19 and how to sign up for ACA benefits.

Setting a Standard

"Setting a standard" refers to government mandating a requirement that all citizens or businesses must meet. During the COVID-19 pandemic, many of these standards were enacted at the state level and ran the spectrum from masks in schools to vaccinations for nursing home workers to social distancing in restaurants. Another example is the federal government setting a minimum wage of $7.25 but allowing states and some local governments to establish rates higher than the federal floor. For example, Oregon has a minimum wage of $12.75; Arizona's minimum wage is $12.15. Both the federal government and states hire staff to investigate noncompliance and fine those firms that abuse the system.

The federal government sets many standards in the environmental area, as well. For example, in 2011, it adopted the first standard on mercury, arsenic and other toxic emissions from power plants. Also, the U.S. Department of Commerce Occupational Safety and Health Administration sets numerous standards for worker safety and health. Some standards are encoded in law; others are encoded in agency rules and regulations.

Moderate Policies

Most potential new policies fall between the incremental changes discussed earlier and bolder, more interventionist policies. They are in the middle of the spectrum in terms of their likelihood to be adopted and implemented. Essentially, these policies are most often amendments to laws, rules, regulations, executive orders and other guidance. That said, there are times when they can be new, stand-alone laws.

Laws

The adoption of a new policy often means enacting a new law at the federal or state level, and most new major initiatives require this. Thus, the legislature must pass the proposed legislation, and the president or governor must sign it. Given that we have reached a certain maturity level with comprehensive laws at all three levels of government, however, new policy typically amends existing law. It is important to note that in any discussion of policy, you must clarify whether you are proposing a new stand-alone initiative or amendment of existing law. If amending an existing law, discuss that law in the "setting the stage" section of the report.

Rules and Regulations

It is also true that many laws require the agency of jurisdiction to promulgate new rules and regulations that provide additional guidance on how the program will be administered, including how the law will be enforced. That said, existing rules and regulations can be updated at any time, and totally new rules can be promulgated as long they have a basis in law. A "rule" provides broad direction on a major provision of the law, while a "regulation" gets into specific interpretations or nitty-gritty guidance. A single rule often includes several hundred regulations.

Rules and regulations essentially have the strength of a law because they are implementing the law. That said, they can be overturned by the courts if they conflict with the state or federal constitution or existing laws. Separate laws provide guidelines on how rules are promulgated. At the federal level, the Office of Management and Budget (OMB) must approve each new rule or regulation, and it performs a cost-benefit analysis on most of them. At the state level, the budget office also plays a coordinating roll. There is typically a requirement to provide notice (e.g., in the Federal Register) and include a public comment period before the rule is promulgated. Finally, the rule or regulation must be consistent with the underlying law.

In terms of potential policy changes, an entire rule is seldomly repealed and reissued. Such change is more likely to happen for a specific regulation. The likeliest scenario is that a law is amended, and then a new rule is promulgated or a specific regulation is repealed and reissued.

Executive Orders

Over time, as both political parties have become increasingly reluctant to come together on bipartisan legislation, presidents and governors alike have used their authority to issue executive orders, or proclamations that establish policy. These orders were used at the federal level as far back as our first president, George Washington. The orders are not referenced in the U.S. Constitution or most state constitutions, but defenders often interpret the basis as being implied in some provisions. In all cases, they have the force of law, even though neither the legislature nor the judiciary may be consulted. They can, however, be overturned by the courts or the legislature. Given that they have been used by both presidents and governors for so long, there is now a strong precedent that they will continue.

Guidance

Federal and state agencies provide more informal guidance in interagency statements, advisories, Q&As and FAQ documents. These are all helpful, but they are not binding; neither do they have the force of law. Although they can, they generally do not go through the formal process for rules and regulations. For the Medicaid program, the federal government has issued thousands of letters of guidance since the program's enactment in 1965.

Bolder, More Interventionist Policies

Historically in the United States, many bold legislative actions have been transformative, such as the Federal Aid Highway Act of 1958, the Civil Rights Act of 1964, Medicare and Medicaid in 1965 and the Clean Air Act

Amendments of 1970. More recently, the ACA could be added to the list.

At the state level, the California Air Pollution Control Act of 1947 was a bold new approach that established 58 control districts and most likely contributed to the enactment of clean air legislation at the federal level, including the 1970 amendments. Similarly, the Massachusetts health care reform act of 2006 essentially established universal health care in the state. Although it is not necessary, most of these actions were fiscally significant policies that had major impacts on the spending and revenue of both the state and federal governments. They also tend to be more interventionist in terms of markets and therefore create more inefficiency. Often, these initiatives are comprehensive and complex and include major new mandates and regulations as well as new programs and taxes.

Spending

Any expansion of an existing federal, state or local government program generally requires increased appropriation. If the expansion is larger than the current authorization level in law, then the authorization will have to be amended and the appropriation increased. If the program is totally new, it will need both an authorization and an appropriation. The one exception to this pattern is a change in an entitlement or other mandatory program. Here, the authorizing legislation automatically creates funding.

Authorizing laws traditionally set a specific authorization level or states "such sums as necessary." If it sets a level (e.g., $300 million), then the appropriation total must be $300 million or less. Often, the authorizing legislation sets a level substantially above what the eventual appropriation will be. If the authorizing legislation does not include a total, then it is usually up to the OMB at the federal level or the state budget or legislative office to create a reasonable cost estimate. At the federal level, the appropriations committee will provide budget authority, which is the amount available to spend and an estimate of spending, called "outlays." The outlay estimates are based on similar programs. Programs that are mostly wages and salaries spend out in outlays quickly over a year or two, while capital projects, such as highways, may spend out over the next seven years. Programs generally require an appropriation for staffing and other costs to administer a new program or service. It could also be for a grant program, such as for state governments to implement a program such as Medicaid, or they could be housing subsidies, such as Section 8, or a new benefit program for child care. Also, the federal government also often funds loan programs, such as student loans, where they must provide sufficient funding to cover administrative costs and defaults.

Taxes

Some taxes are primarily used to create behavioral changes, such as reducing smoking or alcohol consumption. Other taxes are essentially to raise revenues in general or to fund a specific new program or expand an existing program. Sometimes, the revenue is legally dedicated to a particular program, such as federal gasoline taxes being dedicated to highway and bridge construction and repair. At the federal level, there are often several hundred dedicated revenues or trust funds. Tax changes must start with the Ways and Means Committee in the U.S. House of Representatives, but they must also go through the Finance Committee in the U.S. Senate. A similar situation exists at the state level in that most states have finance committees that have jurisdiction over all revenue bills. If the tax increases are to fund a large new program, significant coordination problems may arise as the spending and revenue bills go through different committees at different times.

A Final Comment

If you follow the approach outlined in this chapter, start with a broad set of different policies, with at least one policy that has the goal of making the market work and at least one nontraditional policy. You should also have at least one policy that is incremental, a couple that are moderate, and one bold intervention policy. So, your first draft should include a group of about six policies in addition to current policy. You will likely end up with three or four policies in addition to current policy over time, but six is still a good starting point. Avoid selecting several policies that are similar. Policies will drop out because they are not workable or there is little evidence of success by other governments. You may also learn that some policies are just not politically feasible.

Chapter 5
Developing the Criteria

In the political world, the debate is primarily about political feasibility and costs. By "costs," we typically mean government or budget costs, not total social costs, which is the appropriate measure of cost-effectiveness. Costs often influence political feasibility, largely because in U.S. House of Representatives and Senate rules require that all bills have a cost estimate from the Congressional Budget Office before being voted on for final passage. Estimates are not required for votes at the committee level. In addition, the congressional budget process is complex and often creates obstacles for funding. The budget processes in most states is simple although many also require a fiscal note before final passage of bills.

Although you should tailor the criteria to your problem, five core criteria should generally be part of most evaluations:

- Political feasibility.
- Likelihood of being financed.
- Ease of implementation.

- Equity.
- Cost-effectiveness.

Political Feasibility

Make sure that the policy you are considering has some chance of being adopted. It could be an executive order from a governor or the president or a rule or regulation that is promulgated by the agency secretary or by a commission. Further, it could be a bill approved by the legislature and signed by the governor or the president that creates a new law or amends an existing one. It is important to specify the adopting entity in each policy.

Next, differentiate the actual decision-makers from outside groups and stakeholders that could influence the final decision. For example, most states deciding whether to expand eligibility for Medicaid under the Patient Protection and Affordable Care Act (ACA) must do so by enacting a new law. In this example, the key decision-makers are likely to be the governor, the cabinet secretary who oversees Medicaid, the committee chairs who have jurisdiction in the legislature and perhaps the majority and minority leaders. That said, other senior committee members have powerful voices and thus are often part of the consensus. Outside groups in this case would be the health insurance companies, hospitals, physicians and other health care groups as well as the many advocate organizations for low-income residents. The players will differ across states, and so you must determine them on a case-by-case basis. For example, in some states, teachers' groups are powerful; in other states, it may be ranch or farm groups.

In determining the political feasibility of a policy, research how potential decision-makers have voted on similar issues in the past, and track down any press releases on the bills or specific statements in press conferences they have made on the issue at hand. Similarly, identify a metric to measure the relative importance of other interested groups.

Likelihood of Being Financed

In the U.S. Congress as well as in state and local government, program authorizations and appropriations are separate actions initiated by separate committees, often on separate time schedules. An authorization can create a new program; provide additional authorities; or mandate that state or local government or the private sector do something, such as report on certain activities. Authorizations can take place at any time through any committee. To fund a program, however, an appropriation must be included in an appropriation bill, which generally takes place just once each year. If a new authorization just makes a few tweaks to an existing program, then the assumption is that the agency will shift some resources from other functions to the new one and forego a request for additional funding. In contrast, if the authorization creates a major new benefit program or substantially expands the responsibility of an existing agency, then it generally would require some additional funding through an appropriation.

At other times, a new tax or fee would be created to fund the new program.

Other differences at the federal, state and local government levels affect funding. State and local governments have balanced-budget requirements, which often create pressure not to fund new authorizations. The federal government has no such balanced-budget requirement, but the entire process is more complicated because of the role of budget and appropriations committees. All these pressures mean that it is generally more difficult to get funding at all three levels of government than to pass an authorization bill. It is also true that new executive orders or rules or regulations generally do not receive funding. It is generally assumed this is just part of the normal business of the agency, but this is not always true because additional staff may be required to enforce major new rules or regulations.

Ease of Implementation

One challenge in any legislation is deciding which provisions should be written into law and which should be handled by the agency promulgating the rules. An agency should be able to make changes to accommodate shifting demographics, economics, technology and science. Otherwise, the act in question could become obsolete quickly. In contrast, too much flexibility could allow the next administration to gut the law through regulatory changes. For this and other reasons, potential implementors should have seats at the table while the legislation is being written. Unfortunately, implementation is often an afterthought today, which is why programs and laws often fail.

It is also important to establish metrics for determining the degree of risk in implementation. Perhaps most important is the degree of support or ownership among the staff leading the implementation. The bureaucracy needs to be on board; otherwise, they will slow the process and create obstacles. For example, it is likely that U.S. Immigration and Customs Enforcement staff were more supportive of immigration changes that President Trump advocated than those by President Biden. There is also a need for staff with various levels and areas of expertise— for example, experts to communicate with the public and to liaise with industry groups. For example, in the implementation of the ACA, expertise in health insurance was critical because the private sector insurance companies would be selling health insurance policies in the state and federal marketplace exchanges. Increasingly, the lack of technology expertise in government is a problem, as illustrated during ACA implementation. (See Chapter 8 for a more in-depth discussion of implementation.) For large, complex laws that involve multiple agencies across government, effective coordination is also often a serious obstacle.

Finally, implementation requires a detailed plan and timelines as well as a "Plan B" should serious obstacles appear. All these elements must be vetted extensively and achieve strong consensus by the staff. If implementation is at the federal level, then effective coordination between the lead agency and the White House is critical. Also, given that most domestic programs are run by states, federal-state coordination is critical. (See "Appendix E. Federal-State Coordination.") Further, although individuals with public policy and political experience are generally not the most effective people to lead implementation teams, they are often the ones in charge.[10]

Equity

Equity has become an important criterion. Several different dimensions of equity may exist across income groups, age groups, sex/gender, race and region. Unfortunately, it is difficult to incorporate multiple equity-related issues into an outcome matric. Therefore, you should discuss in your capstone paper three or four major equity issues, define which is most important, and then specify a metric for measuring it.

As an example of a possible equity issue from the problem statement, "The New York state prison system is too expensive." Here one of the most important equity issues is between the prisoners and the guards, who generally live in the communities surrounding the prisons. Some policies that give parole boards more flexibility to allow early release of prisoners also led to reductions in the number of jobs for guards. Specify the equity between two

---

[10] Cutler, D. (2010, May 11). *Urgent need for changes in health reform implementation.* Memo to Larry Summers. https://policymemos.hks.harvard.edu/files/policymemos/files/sol e_borras_memo.pdf?m=1610655476

groups in your analysis, include it in the outcome metric and measure it to the extent possible. For example, you could develop metrics such as the income guards lost relative to the income prisoners gained.

Cost-Effectiveness

In most situations, cost-effectiveness is by far the most important criterion because it is the ultimate measure of efficiency. All other criteria need metrics or qualitative measures so that at least an ordinal ranking can be developed, but cost-effectiveness must be calculated so that a numeric measure is available.

Often, the actual efficiency measure may not be obvious. You need to make several early decisions before calculating the measure. First, state the region of impact (it should already be part of your problem statement). For example, if the problem statement is, "Too many rent-burdened individuals are living in Richmond, Virginia," then the costs apply only to residents living in Richmond. Second, determine the actual government that will be the focus. It should be consistent with the geographic region. Third, determine the future time frame over which outcome and cost projections will be made. The period depends on the type of program you are analyzing. If the program is small, focused on a limited number of eligible recipients and easy to administer and modify, then five to eight years into the future would work. At the other extreme, if the decision has to do with a major capital investment, such as a transit or rail system, then you may be talking about a 30-

year or longer time frame. For the average state or federal program, a 10-year period is sufficient. The time horizon must be long enough for the new program to run efficiently and have available performance measures. From enactment, it takes three to four years to plan and implement a new program, and then several more years before the program matures and becomes efficient.

Forth, determine the base year which is generally the most recent year which has actual data. Fifth, determine the outcome and project it over the selected time period for the status quo and all alternatives. It will become the denominator in the cost-effectiveness equation. Essentially, you use the following equation to measure cost-effectiveness.

Cost Effectiveness = Discounted cost over X future Years/Sum of the outcomes over X future years.

"Discounted cost over X future years" refers to all social costs, so it includes government direct spending, economic costs as well as the cost of externalities such as highway congestion and carbon dioxide emissions on the residents of the designated region.

Sixth, from this base year, you calculate all costs for each year in the baseline or status quo policy as well as for all alternative policies. These totals are then discounted at an assumed rate—for example, 3%. This estimate becomes the numerator in the above equation. Finally, you then compare each ratio to the ratio for the status quo to determine the most cost-effective alternative. The next chapter provides detailed steps for calculating cost-effectiveness.

Other Important Criteria

These previously discussed five criteria form the core or your analysis, but you may want to incorporated others, as well. The sections that follow provide some examples.

Political Sustainability

In today's increasingly political world, newly elected presidents, governors and mayors often defund, substantially modify or repeal policies enacted by previous administrations. These actions create substantial inefficiencies in the operation of government programs at all levels. They also create uncertainty for residents and reduce trust in government. A vivid example is Republicans' efforts to repeal the ACA over the past 10 years. It has also played out in numerous court challenges, such as National Federation of Independent Business v. Sebelius,[11] and in the floor vote where U.S. Sen. John McCain of Arizona famously broke with his party and voted against the repeal on July 27, 2017. If the ACA had been repealed, it would have been a costly disruption to health for millions of American families. The ACA was vulnerable

---

[11] National Federation of Independent Business v. Sebelius, No. 11–393 (2012). https://www.law.cornell.edu/wex/national_federation_of_indepe ndent_business_v._sebelius_(2012)

in part because the Democrats enacted it though reconciliation without a single Republican vote in either the House of Representatives or the Senate. In 2017, during the Trump presidency, the Republicans passed a major tax cut with no Democrat support in either chamber. Similarly, when Biden was elected president, he repealed many of President Trump's executive orders on immigration and the environment. He would have repealed or modified many provisions in the Trump 2017 tax bill, as well, had he had the votes.

Similar disruptions happen quite often in state and local governments. For example, newly elected Virginia Gov. Glenn Youngkin issued an executive order on Jan. 15, 2022, that rescinded the previous governor's mask mandates for COVID-19.

Because of the potential impacts that repeal of various laws imposes on citizens, it may be better to pursue incremental policy changes that have bipartisan support. That said, including sustainability among your criteria may result in better policy recommendations.

Quality

For some analyses, such as those focused on the high cost of health care, it may be important to include a quality measure among your criteria. In the 1990s, the rapid expansion of managed care revolutionized health care. For several years, policymakers applauded how this shift stabilized the share of income Americans spent on health care premiums. Then, the backlash came from physicians, hospitals and patients when consumers lost access to their existing doctors and were denied payment for recommended procedures. Insurance companies didn't manage care, they reduced the access to quality care in order to reduce costs. Including quality of care as one of the criteria helps to guard against faulty analysis.

Take, for example, the Healthcare Effectiveness Data and Information Set (HEDIS),[12] which is widely used as a quality measure. When quantifying the effectiveness of care of a given provider, HEDIS uses a complex measure of effectiveness of care, incorporating variables such as body mass index, blood pressure and presence of substance use to fully assess the health of the provider's patients. HEDIS also offers scores for the accessibility of health care services, which includes measures of adults' access to ambulance services and dental coverage and the availability of pediatric services. Generally, patients and families can use this information to evaluate insurance providers. Quality measures also exist for nursing homes, including metrics on safety (e.g., the number of deficiencies found during an inspection), on effectiveness (e.g., weight loss) and timeliness (e.g., how quickly patient calls were answered).

As the nation has moved to value in health care through accountable care organizations, new quality measures have been created. Be sure to review the literature and decide which measures of quality fit the problem you are analyzing.

---

[12] National Committee for Quality Assurance. (n.d.). *HEDIS measures and technical resources.* Retrieved June 10, 2021, from https://www.ncqa.org/hedis/measures/

Proficiency

For some public schools, the public policy issue is high dropout rates; for others, it may be poor academic performance. Unfortunately, for many schools, both are a problem. If you are analyzing elementary and secondary schools, including proficiency among your criteria helps guard against policies that reduce dropout rates by lowering education standards.

For example, when thinking about proficiency in education, policymakers have used standardized testing as an extremely useful metric for determining gains and losses in a school's academic performance. Many states administer their own standardized tests. For instance, Virginia administers the Standards of Learning test[13] to students in elementary school. Some state examinations provide good measures of proficiency, but many more are biased and show overly high rates of proficiency. For this reason, it is difficult to compare performance across states. Fortunately, the federal government requires that states also administer the National Assessment of Educational Progress (NAEP)[14] for a sample number of students in 4th, 8th and 12th grades to track educational attainment. This is a much higher-quality test which is comparable across states. Although standardized tests such as these have been

---

[13] Virginia Department of Education. (n.d.). *Standards of Learning (SOL) and Testing.* Retrieved June 10, 2021, from https://www.doe.virginia.gov/testing/index.shtml

[14] National Center for Education Statistics. (n.d.). *About the nation's report card.* Retrieved June 10, 2021, from https://nces.ed.gov/nationsreportcard/about/

criticized for failing to capture the whole aptitude of an individual student, the scores are incredibly useful in assessing the quality of education for specific public-school systems. The downside of the NAEP test is that only a sample of students take it, and the data are for three years only. It can, however, be used to adjust the individual state tests and make them comparable.

There may be other possible criterion such as the impact on a community, animal habitat or civil rights, but be sure to limit the number of criteria in your report to not more than six as any more will make the analysis unwieldly. Always start with the five core criteria, and reject one of them only in special circumstances. Given our current partisan political environment, it may be wise to include political sustainability. Add the quality criterion only when the risks of reducing quality are high.

It is also important to develop relative weights for your chosen criteria. Cost-effectiveness generally should receive the greatest weight—often 50% or more, depending on the quality of the estimates. Next in importance is political feasibility. Tailor the remaining weights to the specific issue you are analyzing.

Chapter 6
Estimating Cost-Effectiveness

This chapter begins by identifying the four decisions you must make before you can calculate cost-effectiveness measures. It then proposes an overall projection methodology for generating back-of-the-envelope estimates of cost-effectiveness for policy alternatives. The rest of the chapter details the eight steps to measuring cost-effectiveness. These measures are critical because cost-effectiveness is the only criterion for which you provide quantitative rather than qualitative measures. In the policy world, costs are a dominant consideration and thus traditionally are given a weight of at least 50% in the outcomes matrix.

The Four Early Decisions

Before you can calculate cost-effectiveness, you must decide on four elements: (1) the outcome (2) the base year (3) the region and (4) the time horizon. These elements are critical and are part of analytical framework of your report.

The Outcome

First and most important, what is the outcome measure? Essentially, the outcome is what an individual program should maximize in public policy. Outcome differs from output, which is merely a measure of what has been produced from a program and does not address the value or impact of the service or program. Instead, the outcome includes a level of performance or achievement. It is a physical measure, such as the number of individuals with health insurance or the tons of carbon dioxide or the number of homeless people in a given geography, not generally is it a value or dollar amount. This critical measure is used in the denominator in your calculation of cost-effectiveness, and it must be consistent with your problem statement.

The data series you use must align with the correct concept, of your outcome. For example, three different concepts exist for income: before taxes, after taxes and after taxes plus transfer payments. If you are developing measures of the number of individuals who are health care or housing cost burdened, then you want the "after tax with transfers" measures because it is the best measure of actual discretionary income. If, however, your interest is in determining appropriate tax policy income, "before taxes" may be the most appropriate measure.

The Base Year

The second decision you must make is your base year. This year should be the last year for which you have actual data for both your outcome and your costs. This year is particularly important for your cost determination because you will need to pull data from at least several different sources.

When you have identified your base year, you then assume a freeze all policies, including existing laws, rules and regulations, at that point. Similarly, you will assume that the rate of change in technology is the historical change going forward from this year. To accommodate lags in reporting data, the base year for most projects is typically two to three years before the date of writing your report.

The Region

Third, determine the region your analysis will cover. Every analysis Is done for a specific geographic region, such as a country, a state, a city or a county. You will evaluate the social costs on residents of that region. Generally, the region is the same as the jurisdiction of the government under analysis.

The Time Horizon

Finally, decide how far into the future you must look to develop a valid analysis. This determination will depend on the type of program under consideration. For large capital investments, such as highways, power plants and similar infrastructure, a 20- to 30-year time frame is likely best. Such investments may last longer than that, but beyond 30 years, estimates become highly speculative.

If, however, you are considering a simple, small program, such as a mentoring program that can be adopted and implemented quickly, then a five- to eight-year timetable could work. Most programs can be implemented and reach a level of efficiency within a ten-year time frame. You want a period long enough that you can determine whether the program is meeting its outcome and cost goals.

The Methodology

Occasionally, there may be sufficient time to create sophisticated and reliable projection methodologies—either because the policy initiative is large and comprehensive, or because the projections must be repeated annually. In these large efforts, models are developed that have many simultaneous equations, with independent and dependent variables, such as those of the Office of Management and Budget (OMB) and the Congressional Budget Office. Moody's Analytics does the same at the state level with its regional models for projecting Gross Domestic Product by State and other economic variables.

More often, calculations in the public policy arena are back-of-the-envelope estimates. These rough approximations work for two reasons. First, there is generally no time to develop a more sophisticated approach. If you do have additional time, then you should use those more sophisticated approaches to estimate variables. Second, most analysts do not have access to the high-quality data the better approaches require. Therefore, the best strategy is often to make an initial cut using the simple approach; then, if the quality of the underlying data is good and you have time, substitute alternative approaches for the most important variables.

The simplest projection methodology is to use the historical average growth rate over the preceding 10 to 15 years and assume that it will remain constant in the future. Other simple approaches include exponential smoothing, which weighs recent observations more heavily, or a simple time series regression. Alternatively—and this is the projection methodology this guide advocates—determine the historical relationship between your outcome or cost variable and the related economic or demographic variables that are projected by the federal government or other research organizations known for doing high-quality projections. Then apply that historical relationship to the future projections by these organizations.

Most variables are related to the underlying growth in population or a particular age cohort of that population growth. For example, if you are attempting to project the number of students enrolled in high school in Richmond, Virginia, then you would first quantify the historical relationship between the number of individuals 12 to 18 years of age from population estimates and school enrollment. You would then apply this historical relationship to the U.S. Census Bureau projections for that age cohort of 12 to 18 for the ten future years. That historical relationship is generally stable, so the method provides good final projections. Other than population, many outcomes can be linked to employment or gross product in a region.

Assumptions

Throughout your analysis, you will need to make numerous assumptions because little reliable data are available. Distinguish between those variables that will have a major impact on your final recommendation and those that will not. For example, an assumption regarding the extent to which the outcome will change in the future for each alternative relative to current policy is a critical assumption and one for which you should conduct substantial research in advance. In contrast, an assumption about the percentage of direct salary and wage compensation represented by health care, pension and vacation benefits is far less important, particularly because you would use the same percentage for all the alternatives you propose. This distinction is important in terms of your time allocation for the report.

Informed Judgment and Data

Keep in mind that the best reports reflect a combination of research and effective use of the data you uncover while making informed decisions regarding assumptions. As indicated previously, you should maintain contact with individuals who have in-depth knowledge of the issue under analysis as well as (in the case of existing programs) those currently administering the program. These individuals will be invaluable in helping you develop assumptions.

Push Forward

When it comes to performing quantitative analysis, students often feel overwhelmed and thus do not know where to start. Start by pulling together the historical information you need, particularly for outcome series, for which data are generally more widely available. It may be easier to focus on the base year costs, and then the projections of both outcomes and costs. However you decide to start, I encourage you to push forward and just do it so that you have sufficient time to review and modify your estimates. The eight steps that follow will help you calculate the cost-effectiveness of your proposed policy.

Eight Steps for Calculating Cost-Effectiveness

This section divides the approach to calculating cost-effectiveness into eight steps. For each step, there is a short discussion of potential methodologies, with examples for how estimates could be derived.

Step 1. Project the Outcome for Current Policy

Begin by pulling together the historical data on the outcome for the most recent 10 to 15 years. In all cases, choose data from primary rather than secondary sources. In general, the best primary source is the federal government—in particular, the Bureau of Labor Statistics, the U.S. Department of Commerce and the U.S. Census Bureau. These agencies' data are often reconciled with other series, making them most reliable. Next, gather data published by state governments. When you need to use other sources, determine the reliability of the data by researching how a series was collected and published.

Next, look at the series to determine whether to drop any abnormal observations. For example, the year 2021 was uniquely affected by the COVID-19 pandemic; thus, you may want to exclude or appropriately weigh observations from this period. Similarly, the great recession of 2009 significantly affected most economic variables, including GDP and employment for both 2009 and 2010; thus, you may want to drop these observations. Judge the extent to which any given observation is an outlier from the underlying trend. Your analysis should focus on long-term trends, not short-term changes. If the final series shows steady but slow growth, it may be possible to assume that the historical growth rate will continue. Alternatively, you can look at the relationship of the outcome relative to population or some specific cohort of population over the previous 10 to 15 years, and then apply that historical relationship to the population projections for the region under analysis.

The U.S. Census Bureau publishes high-quality population projections, with substantial detail regarding age, sex, race and region. In addition, most states have an office on demographics, often at a state university or college, that provides further population detail for political regions in the state that are consistent with Census Bureau projections. State legislatures often use these data to allocate federal and state aid to substate governments. In Virginia, this work is done by the Weldon Cooper Center at the University of Virginia. As an example of using population, assume that the public policy problem is "too few individuals in the state of Maryland receive a four-year college degree." To project the current policy, you would first determine the historical percentage of the cohort of people 20 to 26 years of age who graduate each year. If this percentage is relatively constant, then you could assume that there would be little change in the future. From there, you could apply this percentage to the population projection of 20- to 26-year-olds in the state of Maryland for 10 years into the future. If, however, there is a trend in the percentage in the historical period, then you could project that trend and apply it to the population projections. Given that most population projections will be only for every five years, you may have to interpolate individual years by assuming constant growth rates between the five-year periods. If no good relationship exists between the outcome and the population, then determine whether there is a better relationship to some economic measure, such as GDP or Gross Domestic Product by State. It is also possible that the relationship is better between population and a component of GDP, such as personal consumption expenditures.

Another approach is to use a more formal approach, such as a time series regression or regression relative to some of these economic variables or an exponential smoothing technique that weighs the most recent observations more heavily. In general, I recommend using a couple of approaches; then, you can compare results to make a final decision. The final projection might be based on any one of the three approaches or on a small adjustment to one of the series based on the other two.

Step 2. Project the Outcomes for All Other Policy Alternatives

For these other alternatives, review the evidence or impacts for similar policies from other cities, states or countries. The best studies are ex post facto studies, where a researcher looked back as many as five to 10 years to determine the response rate or change in the outcome after a new policy was enacted. For example, a best-case scenario may be that a new high school mentoring program reduced the number of dropouts by 1% during the first and second years, but then reduced the number of dropouts to 2%, 3%, and then 4% relative to the current policy in years three through five. If this mentoring program is similar to one of your alternative policies, then you could apply this information directly to the current policy to derive the outcome measure projection for that alternative.

If, however, a researcher has made ex ante facto estimates for another city or state for a similar mentoring program, that researcher may have estimated only one or two points on the 10-year time horizon. For example, the study may have indicated that in the fourth year after enactment, dropouts would decline by 3.5% relative to the baseline. Clearly, the data from the ex post facto study are superior to the ex-ante facto study and thus should be used to the extent possible. In both cases, the evidence gives you at best several observations out of the 10 required—or, more likely, only one year of the 10 years you need. In both cases, you will need to make assumptions regarding the remaining estimates for 10 future years. The only evidence available about new programs is that during the first several years after enactment, the outcome does not change much and may even witness reductions for a couple of years as the team that administers the program makes incremental changes to improve efficiency. After the first couple of years, you often see increases in the outcome of several percent per year relative to the baseline only to see it level off, with little change in the last few years of the projection as the program matures.

In public policy, seldom will you have the data you need to project 10 years into the future. Therefore, be prepared to make assumptions so that you can develop the full 10 years based on trends seen in many new initiatives.

Step 3. Develop the Cost for the Base Year for Current Policy

Again, the cost concept here is for total social costs in the geographic region under analysis that is consistent with the government entity under consideration.[15] Given that there are usually existing government programs focused on the problem under analysis, a good starting point is government spending on these programs in the base year you have identified. These are direct, observable costs that you can generally find in federal, state and local government budgets. In all cases, you want the actual spending for the base year, not spending that the president, governor or mayor has proposed.

---

[15] For a good explanation of costs and an example, see Riegg Cellini, S., and Kee, J. E. (2015). Cost-effectiveness and cost-benefit analysis. In Wholey, J. S., Hatry, H. P., and Newcomer, K. E. (Eds.), *Handbook of practical program evaluation.* (3rd ed., pp. 493–530). Wiley.

At the federal level, the term "outlays" is used in place of "spending," while at the state or local level, you will see "spending" or "expenditures." Avoid using "appropriations" or "budget authority," terms generally used to indicate the amount of money made available. Similarly, do not use "obligations," the term used for committed funds.

Costs typically fall into one of seven categories:

- **Actual benefits paid to or on behalf of individuals in a program.** Examples include payments to retired individuals from the Social Security trust funds or Medicare payments made directly to physicians or hospitals.

- **Employee compensation.** Employee compensation includes wages and salaries for staff as well as the costs for benefits such as health care, pensions and vacations for individuals who either administer the existing program or provide oversight. These data are readily available in government budgets.

- **Capital costs.** These costs include the office building, garages and other structures. Yearly cost of structures can be valued in either of two ways. The first is to estimate the depreciation or loss in value of the structure as well as the opportunity cost on the remaining value plus the cost of maintenance. Finding data on these costs may be difficult, so it is better to estimate the average number of square feet each employee uses, then look to the existing real estate rental market to determine a cost per square foot. Estimates that rely on market prices are often far easier to calculate and are more accurate.

- **So-called "overhead costs."** These costs typically include human resources and similar costs for the support staff that are directly related to the program.
- **Direct Purchases including costs of technology support.** Virtually all government programs need to make direct purchases of private sector goods and services. The costs for computers and servers used to be considered a capital cost, but today, due to rapid obsolescence they are considered more of an operations cost. The category includes both the cost of the equipment as well as the staff dedicated to technology support.
- **Costs of externalities.** These are the costs such as air or water pollution and climate change that are imposed on society but are not observable or paid. These have to be estimated by quantifying the number of individuals impacted in the region and the costs imposed. There are numerous high-quality estimates of the costs in the literature. Special care must be exercised in estimating these costs as they may be significant.
- **Economic or Opportunity Costs.** These are lost wages or reductions in GDP due to a health problem or early disability or death. These costs may not be observable.

Let's look at an example of the costs associated with the following problem statement. "People drive too many vehicle-miles in the commonwealth of Virginia." Here, the major costs fall into several categories. First are the yearly capital costs to operate the vehicles in the state, which would include depreciation, and the opportunity costs on the value of the vehicle. It would also include the direct purchases of gasoline and maintenance. Next is the annual capital costs of the state highway and bridge network, including the depreciation on the initial investment, the opportunity costs on the value of the infrastructure and current maintenance costs. A third category is staffing and related costs for those administering the various safety and toll systems in the state's transportation department. Finally, there are two huge externalities you must calculate: carbon dioxide emissions and congestion. In both cases, several studies can help you develop costs per ton of carbon dioxide and costs per hour in congestion.

Step 4. Project the Costs of the Current Policy

Costs will increase over time for one of two reasons: inflation or growth in the outcome. They seldom grow as fast as the outcome because of small incremental increases in productivity, defined as the increase in outcome over and above the increase in all labor and capital inputs. The best way to project costs into the future is to estimate costs for each of the preceding 10 years, as you did for the base year. You would then apply this historical trend growth rate to the future period after determining whether you should drop any observations as outliers.

Other ways to project total costs are to link costs to the number of employees historically, and then independently project the number of employees and the costs per employee. Employee data are generally high quality and easily accessible. Alternatively, you could link total costs to a state economic measure, such as Gross Domestic Product by State, and then use the state's projection and the historical ratio to estimate the costs. You could also link to projections of total employment in a state.

Step 5. Generate the Costs for All Alternative Policies

Two alternative approaches exist for developing costs for each policy alternative. The first is to search the literature for cost estimates for similar programs. For example, in 2000, several states, including Arkansas, Kentucky and Indiana, experimented with work requirements for able-bodied adults in their Medicaid programs. Several studies tracked the information and measured the potential saving to the state as well as the costs of ensure that those enrolled in Medicaid found a job and continued to work a minimum of 20 hours per week. This type of information is often available in the literature and can be used to develop reliable estimates. If no such information is available, you may need to create a cost estimate based on assumptions regarding the number of employees, their compensation, the square footage of office space required and miscellaneous costs. Even here, though, it would be best to rely on data from other governmental programs. When you have estimated and projected these costs, add them to current policy costs for each of the future years. Remember, however, that when a new program is created, an existing one is often sunset. When this happens, be sure to deduct the cost of the eliminated program from the current policy costs.

Step 6. Verify That All Estimates Are Complete

Create and verify estimates for each of the 10 future years (e.g., 2022 through 2033) for the following two series:

- **Outcomes for each of the 10 future years for the base case and the four policy alternatives.** These will be summed, and then become denominators for all cost-effectiveness calculations.
- **Total social costs for each of the 10 future years for the base case and the four policy alternatives.** These costs will become the numerator once they are discounted to generate a net present value (NPV). Assuming one current policy and four alternatives each for ten years into the future means 50 outcome and 50 cost projections, for a total of 100 estimates.

Step 7. Choose a Social Discount Rate

Both cost-benefit and cost-effectiveness measures incorporate a social discount rate. This rate attempts to value the future flow of costs or benefits and convert them to a net present value (NPV). Alternatively, the rate measures what those flows are worth today. Think of the social discount rate like a private rate of return that indicates the current investment needed to receive a flow of revenues in the future. The discount rate is important because it can substantially affect the underlying final measures of cost-effectiveness. This rate depends on several factors, such as the opportunity cost, the inflation rate, the time horizon and especially the risk. Low discount rates are generally estimated at about 3%, while intermediate rates are between 4% and 7% and high rates are above 7%.

A rate often considered riskless is the U.S. Treasury 10-year bond rate, which over the long term has been about 3%. Think of the Treasury bond rate as a minimum rate: The higher the risk and the higher the inflation rate, the higher the discount rate. Similarly, the higher the opportunity cost for the next-best investment, the higher the discount rate. At the federal level, three government agencies conduct considerable cost-benefit and cost-effectiveness analyses and thus tend to set the standard for choosing a social discount rate. The most important agency is the OMB because it works with agencies to perform cost-benefit analyses on all major rules and regulations. OMB publishes Circular A-4, which is updated periodically and includes guidance to agencies on social discount rates. The office recommends two different rates. The first is a 7% rate, which is an estimate of the average before-tax rate of return to private capital in the U.S. economy.[16] It is intended to

---

[16] Council of Economic Advisors. (2017, January). *Discounting for public policy: Theory and recent evidence on the merits of updating the discount rate* (Issue Brief). Obama White House Archives.

approximate the average opportunity cost for capital in the United States. Further, it is based on the long-term rate calculated in the National Income and Product Accounts.

OMB also recommends a 3% rate, which is the real rate of return on long-term government debt. Alternatively, it indicates that it is also the average rate that savers use to discount future consumption. The General Accountability Office (GAO) uses a similar approach in all the analyses it performs for the Congress: "In general, the discount rate for GAO analyses should be the interest on marketable Treasury Debt with maturity comparable to that of the program being evaluated." The Congressional Budget Office, which performs program analysis for the Congress, uses a similar approach. For example, in its analysis of Social Security, the office uses the average interest rate for federal government debt that the Social Security trust fund holds.

Step 8. Generate the Net Present Value for the Current Policy and Each Alternative

Use Microsoft Excel or a similar program to generate the NPV estimates for the current policy and all alternatives. For each alternative, the cost estimates for each of the 10 future years and the assumed discount rate would be inputs into the program, which then generates the NPV for each alternative. Figure 2 is an example of an NPV calculation taken from a publication of the Corporate Finance

---

https://obamawhitehouse.archives.gov/sites/default/files/page/fil es/201701_cea_discounting_issue_brief.pdf

Institute.[17] It shows that the NPV of the cash flow of $10,000 each year over 10 years is $61,466, which means that a rational investor would be willing to pay up to $61,466 to receive the $10,000 every year over 10 years. Although this example is from a private sector investor, the same method is used for cost-effectiveness. Here, it would mean that the NPV of $10,000 in costs for each of 10 future years would be $61,466.

---

[17] Corporate Finance Institute. (n.d.). *Net present value (NPV)*. Retrieved April 11, 2022, from https://corporatefinanceinstitute.com/resources/knowledge/valuation/net-present-value-npv

Discount Rate 10.0%

Year	1	2	3	4	5	6	7	8	9	10
Discount Factor	0.91	0.83	0.75	0.68	0.62	0.56	0.51	0.47	0.42	0.39
Undiscounted Cash Flow	10,000	10,000	10,000	10,000	10,000	10,000	10,000	10,000	10,000	10,000
Present Value	9,091	8,264	7,513	6,830	6,209	5,645	5,132	4,665	4,241	3,855

Net Present Value 61,446

Figure 2. Example of a Net Present Value Calculation from the Private Sector

Step 8. Calculate Cost-Effectiveness Measures

The final step in the calculation is to determine the cost-effectiveness measures for the current policy and each alternative policy. Sum the outcomes over the 10 years for each policy, then divide the sums into the NPVs for each policy. Interpret these estimates as the total discounted social cost per unit of outcome. Depending on your problem statement and outcome, this might mean the cost of one dropout prevented or the cost of one rent-burdened person reduced. Include these final estimates in the outcomes matrix of your final policy recommendation.

High-Quality Projections

This section summarizes some of the high-quality projections you can use to project outcomes or costs based on the historical relationship between these variables and your outcome or cost.

U.S. Census Bureau Population Projection

The U.S. Census Bureau routinely publishes long-term projections of the U.S. population, the most comprehensive of which cover a 55-year period.[18] These long-term publications are published every 10 years and usually updated 2 years after publication. The projections are based

---

[18] U.S. Census Bureau. (2021, October 8). *Population projections.* https://www.census.gov/programs-surveys/popproj.html

on data from the Decennial Census and include data on race, ethnicity, sex and age cohort as well as whether a person is native born or foreign born. The projections also give estimates for how many births and deaths will occur within a given period. The bureau publishes subsequent working papers after the projections, breaking down the population projections by state and exploring a specific topic, such as fertility or employment. Different population projections are published according to immigration scenarios, which are categorized as low, medium and high.

Substate Regional-Level Population Projections

Long-term locality-level population projections are usually developed in a state's academic institutions.[19] These projections are specific to the city or county level and are intended for use by state and local officials, especially for use in funding allocations. The level of detail can vary across reports, with some containing data about employment and race and others limiting data to factors such as sex and age. These population projections depend on research grants awarded by the state. Universities generally provide links to many different facets of their demographics research, such as working papers that summarize their findings, raw data tables available for

---

[19] Demographics Research Group, University of Virginia Weldon Cooper Center for Public Service. (2019). *Virginia population projections.*
https://demographics.coopercenter.org/virginia-population-projections

download and detailed explanations of their methodology. Some even provide data visualizations, such as interactive maps, for ease of use.

Long-Term Gross Domestic Product Projections from the Congressional Budget Office and Office of Management and Budget

Both the Congressional Budget Office and OMB publish their own projections for GDP in the United States every year as part of their budget projections.[20,21] The Congressional Budget Office puts out GDP projections frequently, usually two or three times per year. The White House will publish the President's Budget every fiscal year; this budget contains the OMB GDP projections. Both the Congressional Budget Office and OMB reports contain levels of spending by major program area as well as revenues for each year alongside the GDP projections. Projections cover 10 years into the future for both organizations.

---

[20] Congressional Budget Office. (2021, March). *The 2021 long-term budget outlook.* https://www.cbo.gov/publication/57038

[21] Office of Management and Budget. (n.d.). *Budget of the United States.* Gov.info. Retrieved April 11, 2022, from https://www.govinfo.gov/app/collection/budget

Long-Term Gross Domestic Product Projections from the Organization for Economic Cooperation and Development

The Organization for Economic Cooperation and Development publishes its Economic Outlook report twice every year.[22] This contains projections of GDP for all leading rich and developing nations (Group of 20, or G-20) and for the global economy. Projections cover two years into the future from the publication year. The reports are incredibly detailed, covering labor market trends, inflation, household saving, fiscal trends and shipping cost changes in addition to GDP forecasts. Most of the Economic Outlook report is devoted to trends in the global economy, but for each G-20 nation, the report does give a detailed projection of GDP as well as a summary of major pending legislation predicted to have wide-ranging impacts on economic growth and fiscal standing.

Bureau of Labor Statistics Long-Term Projections (8)

Every year, the Bureau of Labor Statistics publishes a projection of employment trends for the United States.[23] These projections typically cover 10 years. Occasionally,

---

[22] Organization for Economic Cooperation and Development. (n.d.). *Key economic projections by country.* Retrieved April 11, 2022, from

https://www.oecd.org/economy/keyeconomicprojectionsbycountry.htm

[23] U.S Bureau of Labor Statistics. (n.d.). *Employment projections.* Retrieved April 11, 2022, from https://www.bls.gov/emp/

projections are made that cover longer periods. The bureau creates these projections by combining data on labor force participation that it gathers with the U.S. Census Bureau's population projections. The main source of change in the labor force in these projections is the change in population. Changes in labor force participation are provided by age and sex, reflecting children aging into the workforce and seniors either retiring or continuing to work. These reports also contain projections by industry and occupation.

Government Accountability Office Long-Term Budget Projections

The GAO routinely publishes projections of government spending at all levels of government.[24] Studies are usually undertaken in response to the passage of new budgets or major legislation. State and local spending projections can typically be found in separate reports from the federal spending projections. The time horizon for the projections varies significantly, ranging from 10 to 70 years. Projections are specific for major programs or budget function area for the federal government and in select spending areas at the state level. Projections for spending on individual programs in certain states can also be found in individual reports. Local government spending projections are not available. Rather, the GAO reports focus on fiscal environment changes for local governments, usually after a large influx of federal assistance money.

---

[24] General Accountability Office. (2021, March 23). *The nations fiscal health: After pandemic recovery, focus on long-term fiscal sustainability.* https://www.gao.gov/products/gao-21–275sp

Long-Term Gross Domestic Product Projections from Moody's Analytics

Moody's Analytics produces many economic projections for various state and local governments.[25] Projections are available for all U.S. counties, states, metropolitan areas and the country. These projections are available quarterly, and Moody's updates them monthly. They contain projections of GDP, income, employment, prices and demographics at all levels. The projections are developed with alternative scenarios for economic growth.

---

[25] Moody's Analytics. (n.d.). *Economic forecasts.* Retrieved April 11, 2022, from https://www.moodysanalytics.com/solutions-overview/economic/economic-forecasts

Chapter 7
The Recommendation

In this chapter, learn how to bring all the critical information together to make an effective policy recommendation. The chapter describes how to present your outcome matrix, findings and methodology and make your recommendation. It also talks about performing sensitivity analyses and making a secondary recommendation. Finally, it provides examples of how you can incorporate all the information into the final report, including what information should be in appendices.

The Outcomes Matrix

An outcomes matrix is a great way to bring together all the evaluative information you have gathered in one place. Typically, the matrix is a simple table in which the current policy or status quo and your three or four alternative policies appear on the rows and the criteria you developed are the headings of the columns. (See Table 1 for an example.)

Table 1. A Typical Outcomes Matrix

	Cost-effectiveness (40%)	Political Feasibility (20%)	Ease of Implementation (15%)	Equity (25%)
Status quo				
Alternative A				
Alternative B				
Alternative C				

Your preliminary recommendation, as displayed in the outcomes matric, should be based on the quantitative estimates of cost-effectiveness and the metrics you developed for each of the more qualitative criteria as well as the relative weights you have assigned each criterion. Present the qualitative measures in an ordinal ranking of high, medium, and low or 1, 2, 3, 4 (from low to high), depending on the quality of the metrics. Avoid rankings of 1 through 5 or higher because readers may infer more accuracy than what you intend.

Next, confer with the individuals whose advice you have sought throughout the project. Some of these individuals should be experts on the subject at hand; others should have first-hand knowledge of the program under consideration. Hold these discussions in a group setting so that each can hear the others' comments and respond. It is important to focus on potential unintended consequences as part of this discussion. Also, try to avoid being unduly influenced by any one adviser. After this discussion, you should be able to generate your findings and your final recommendation.

Findings

In the "Findings" section, summarize the results from your outcomes matrix. Start by discussing the weights you applied to each criterion. The focus in this section should be on those criteria that have high absolute weights as well as outliers relative to traditional thinking. For example, with some issues, equity is more important because of the publicity surrounding the issue. Alternatively, the implementation criteria may have a high weight because all the options are major, complex initiatives.

Next, summarize the cost-effectiveness measures: They are the only quantitative measures in the matrix. It is important that you interpret the results for your readers. For example, "x" could mean that the cost is $7,367 for each high school dropout prevented or that the cost of each ton of carbon dioxide prevented from being released into the air was $769. It is also helpful in this section to explain why one alternative had such a high cost-effectiveness measure. For example, you could point out that there was evidence in Arkansas, Montana and Iowa that similar programs were extremely effective in helping women get off welfare.

Finally, summarize the qualitative measures for the other criteria. Again, rather than discussing each cell in the matrix, focus on those measures that are particularly high or low and discuss some of the metrics. For example, if political feasibility were ranked high, perhaps follow up and indicate there was a "dear colleague" letter that 51 senators and 225 members of the U.S. House of Representatives signed in support of a bill or explain that the White House issued a statement endorsing the bill. Provide evidence and perspective on the findings, not just a summary of the individual cells in the matrix.

Methodology

Include a short summary of your methodology and the assumptions you made for calculating cost-effectiveness. The first section should define the outcome, the geographic region, the base year for all the costs, the political entity for decisions and the time horizon. Support the decision on the time horizon. Another section should focus on the outcome projections, where you reference the historical series. For each alternatives outcome projection, specify the assumed outcome's responsiveness to the policy relative to the current policy. The major evidence for the responsiveness assumption should reference the specific study in the evidence or "best practice" section of your paper.

Next, summarize the base year cost, with data from the major categories of spending, and explain how you arrived at your cost projections. Finally, include the formula you used so that readers know that costs were discounted to estimate net present value and that you assumed a certain discount rate. You must be able to support the discount rate you assume. Tables on assumptions and spreadsheets on cost-effectiveness measures are generally better included in an appendix.

Walk the Walk

Now that all the work is done and you are the expert, don't be shy: Walk the walk and make a strong recommendation. Support that recommendation by discussing the underling evidence. Your analysis should be as objective as possible, so advocate for your recommendation. Be clear about what the current policy is and what specifically you would change—for example, that a specific provision of a specific current law should be repealed or that a specific amendment should be enacted by the state legislature and signed by the governor or that the secretary of education should issue a new regulation that creates mentoring programs in community colleges. If strong evidence exists for the effectiveness of the recommended policy in another city or state, in include that here.

In your discussion, is important to identify problems with the current policy and explain exactly how your recommended approach would reduce those problems. This is also the time to address how you would fund your recommended approach. Is the existing program an entitlement or other mandatory program so that changing the authorizing language automatically changes the funding level? Alternatively, does the program have an existing appropriation, and if so, does your recommendation require additional funds? If additional funds are necessary, where would they come from? Would it be necessary to cut funding for other programs or raise additional revenues through fees or taxes?

Make sure that the evidence in your outcomes matrix supports your recommendation. If there is a recommendation that the analysis does not support, indicate it. If two alternative policies are close in terms of the outcomes matrix, provide additional details on why you recommend one over the other. If appropriate, you could recommend a couple of alternatives as a package, particularly if the two policies reinforce one another in terms of their impact on the outcome. In general, politicians support policies that are practical, cost-effective and socially acceptable.

Secondary Recommendations

It is often helpful to add one or two secondary recommendations to the major recommendation, in large part because you will have gathered considerable additional information about scope the problem under analysis. Two examples of secondary recommendations are creating a pilot program and the need to gather additional data—that is, you may think that a potential policy would be effective but the data to support it are lacking or there are major concerns regarding unintended consequences. Therefore, you could propose a small regional pilot to generate more information before making a final decision.

History is full successful pilots that have led to more innovative programs. Many have taken place in the Medicaid program under a federal waiver (Section 1115 of the Social Security Act) where state experimentation has been very robust. For example, eligibility for the Medicaid program was originally restricted to single women and children. Several state demonstrations in which married couples were made eligible showed that children of these couples received much better health care because parents were more willing to take them to a physician. In the late 1980s, states experimented with work requirements and increasing funds for education and childcare among the working population, which in combination often resulted in women obtaining better jobs and leaving the welfare rolls.

If quality data are lacking, point that out. Sometimes, the issue is the lag between data collection and reporting. Similarly, it is important to point out other data limitations, such as when data are reported yearly when quarterly reporting is necessary.

Sensitivity Analysis

While there are various types of "Sensitivity analysis" that could be performed for purposes of your analysis, the major questions include: Does the final recommendation change with a discount rate of 7% versus 3%? What if cost-effectiveness has a weight of 33% as opposed to 50%? Essentially, from a policy perspective, all such queries translate into questions of confidence for your recommendation. To the extent that two alternatives are very close, as reflected in the outcomes matrix, sensitivity analysis can be very helpful in choosing your final recommendation as well as describing the confidence in your selection.

Chapter 8
Implementation

The implementation of newly enacted legislation is critical to the success of a program. On May 11, 2010, Harvard health care expert David Cutler wrote a memo to President Obama's National Economic Council Director Larry Summers on the need for changes in implementation of the Patient Protection and Affordable Care Act (ACA).[26] Among other things, Cutler was concerned that the team lacked experience in implementation in general, in delivery system reform and in the technology required for an entirely new system. Cutler made recommendations on how to change implementation at both the White House and HHS.

Cutler's foresight was correct: When the time came for people to sign up for the ACA, the system did not work. The result was a black eye for the entire health care reform initiative. This failure contributed to low public approval ratings, which in turn contributed to Republicans spending

---

[26] Cutler, D. (2010, May 11). *Urgent need for changes in health reform implementation.* Memo to Larry Summers. https://policymemos.hks.harvard.edu/files/policymemos/files/sol e_borras_memo.pdf?m=1610655476

the next decade attempting to repeal the act. In 2010, public support for the ACA was about 42%; it has increased over time, however, and in 2021, it was 56% Many of us can remember Sen. John McCain of Arizona voting against the repeal—and his party—on July 28, 2017. It is not unusual for implementations to run into problems: Implementation is often an afterthought, considered only after the legislation has been enacted. That is a big mistake.

What this story indicates is that:

[P]olicy implementation is not a clear-cut automatic process that occurs as soon as legislation is passed. Policy implementation is not self-executing. In fact, a large number of factors may limit the ability of a government agency to implement a recently enacted law. Rarely will all the obstacles affect any single policy, but all must be considered when designing a policy and translating it into an operating program that provides real services for citizens. Any one of the factors may be sufficient to cause failure or suboptimal performance of a policy. In short, it is much easier to prevent a policy from working than it is to make it effective.[27](2)

Researchers have developed theoretical models for implementation, but none seems to work well across different implementation challenges. Fortunately, six steps—tailored to the situation—can help guide effective implementation:

---

[27] Peters, B. G., and Zittoun, P. (Eds.). (2016). *Contemporary approaches to public policy: Theories, controversies and perspectives.* Palgrave Macmillan; pg. 104.

1. Include key implementation provisions in the proposed legislation.
2. Understand the political and economic context.
3. Choose an experienced leader and a team with appropriate expertise.
4. Develop the Plan.
5. Involve stakeholders.
6. Create a feedback loop to evaluate progress and results.

Include Key Implementation Provisions in the Proposed Legislation

Think about implementation as you are developing the proposed legislation. In the 1970s, a staff member at the Office of Management and Budget always knew the best staff members to implement new laws in every agency. When he determined that a congressional committee was getting serious about new legislation, he would call the committee members to see if they would allow his recommended person (or people, depending on the size of the initiative) to be part of the team that fleshed out the legislation. This approach worked well as the major implementation issues were either addressed in the legislation or at least were planned for by the agency staff, but is seldom used today.

Because most domestic programs today are administered at the state level—for example, the Supplemental Nutrition Assistance Program (SNAP),

TANF and Medicaid—it is critical that state staff be brought in early. Unfortunately this seldom happens today. The bottom line is that whoever will have the responsibility to implement the program, whether at the state or federal level, needs to be at the table when the legislation is at the very early stage of being outlined See Appendix E Federal State Implementation for an example of a well-coordinated implementation.

Funding

It is particularly important to authorize and appropriate sufficient funds early for the implementation of any proposed legislation. If the bill is an entitlement, such as Medicaid or SNAP, then administrative funding is often included as a percentage of the benefit payments. Alternatively, you can include a separate authorization and then an appropriation that provides upfront funding. It is critical that these funds be made available when the legislation is signed by the president or chief executive (in the case of state or local governments). If the proposed legislation is not an entitlement but an authorization, then the authorization level and the appropriation must be sufficient to pay for the implementation. The effective date should be when the legislation is signed so that the work on implementation can start as early as possible.

Rules and Regulations

As part of the process of drafting legislation, you must determine which provisions instruct specific agencies to promulgate which rules or regulations. The law must be able to accommodate potential shifts in the underlying demographics, economic volatility, technology changes and even evolution of the underlying science. For example, if you are working on a state highway bill on safety standards, consider allowing the transportation agency to make changes in the rules regarding electric cars and trucks and especially self-driving vehicles as they become more prevalent. At other times, it may be appropriate for an agency, through new rules, to modify eligibility for entitlement programs when the rate of inflation is high. Generally, any new major legislation will require virtually hundreds of new regulations and other types of guidance. The system works well because it enables the agency involved to make changes to prevent the act's obsolescence. If more of the provisions were in law rather than in regulations, then the act would cease to operate efficiently. Furthermore, it used to be easy to make changes in laws through a technical corrections bill, but in today's partisan world, such changes are far more difficult.

Agencies Involved

The more agencies that have responsibilities in the legislation, the more difficult implementation will be. Thus, minimize the number of agencies involved. Where such limitation is difficult, specify a lead agency to coordinate implementation.

Phasing in the Law

A new law's implementation might be phased in for several reasons. The first reason is to give affected individuals time to adjust and conform to the law. For example, in the ACA, there was a mandate for individuals and families to purchase health insurance. The authors of the law were concerned that young, healthy people would not purchase insurance and thus substantially increase the cost for less healthy people. Thus, they created a tax penalty that began in 2014 for individuals and their dependents that was phased in over three years. The penalty was a dollar amount or percentage of income, whichever was higher. For the first year, the dollar amount was $95 per adult and $47.50 per dependent; it increased to $695 per adult and $347.50 per dependent in 2018. In 2018, the maximum percentage of family income was 2.5%. After that, it was linked to inflation. In late 2017, Congress repealed the provision, effective 2019.

Another reason for phasing a law in is the sheer magnitude of the planning necessary. Here again, a case in point is the ACA. Some of its provisions became effective immediately when the law was enacted in 2010. Others were phased in over the next four years, including the creation of exchanges with subsidies for those who qualify, expansion of Medicaid and minimum standards for insurance plans.

Evaluation

An evaluation system should be built into the original law and be part of the implementation. The proposed law should specify the type of data that should be collected and how the evaluation should be done. It is critical to know early if a new law is meeting its outcome goal.

Depending on the ultimate legislative proposal, there may be a lot of media and public interest in the effective date on which some provisions will become operational. These dates should not be set until there is certainty regarding funding and the governing agency's ability to meet that date. It is best not to include the date in the enacted bill but rather leave it to the agency.

Understand the Political and Economic Context

The proposed legislation was developed within a certain historical, social, cultural, political and economic context. Although historical, social and cultural norms generally change slowly, rapid change does occasionally take place. That said, the political and economic environment tends to remain in flux. There can be swings in the national mood, unexpected election results, administration changes, shifts in partisan or ideological views or interest group pressures. Economic downturns take place, as well, such as the so-called "great recession" of 2008–9, when unemployment peaked at 10.0% in October 2009. The entire implementation team—not just its leader—must be in touch with these changes and their potential impacts. It is not unusual for events that seem completely unrelated to the implementation to change the environment. The team should continue to discuss these potential changes in key meeting and, if necessary, develop alternative plans.

Choose an Experienced Leader and Team with Appropriate Expertise

It is important to have a leader who is experienced in implementation and is politically sophisticated. This leader would help the political liaisons brief the White House and senior members of Congress. This person should help maintain the support of all stakeholders and the public. Remember that groups will continue to oppose the legislation; these groups know that they have a second chance to erode public support if the act is poorly implemented.

Success also requires a team with different types of expertise, and a team whose members all agree with the policy—or at least do not oppose it. If the team does not have ownership of the new policy, implementation could slow down, as often happens when the policy was adopted by one administration, then implemented by another after an election. The expertise the team needs will differ depending on the policy, but teams generally should include:

- **Outreach experts.** These individuals will work with the major stakeholders. They often have previous experience working with the groups involved and have a thorough understanding of the legislation's impacts on the stakeholders. Some outreach experts should come the private sector, such as insurance companies, hospitals and physician groups in the case of the ACA, while others could come from state and local governments.

- **Political liaisons.** Liaisons are staff members who have Capitol Hill experience and will work to answer questions from members and committee staff on the Hill. Another group will play a key role in keeping the White House up to speed on the progress of implementation. Both groups must be frank and truthful in explaining the status and challenges of the implementation. Continued political support is crucial to maintaining momentum for effective implementation. The relationship with the White House is always the most challenging aspect of implementation because White House staff generally do not fully trust those in the various agencies.

- **Media experts.** It is important to keep the media and public informed, it is not appropriate to give the media information beyond what is necessary. That said, there should be a constant flow of information that has been extensively vetted. Otherwise, the media may focus on rumors, of which there are often many and many of which are often wrong. Media experts must strike the appropriate balance.

- **Technology experts.** Technology is a special case: Governments do not purchase or implement technology effectively, and so it is often the area with the highest risk. Technology was clearly a major problem in the ACA implementation. The first problem is the long process in government for providing technology funding. A technology plan must first be developed, then priced out to determine the cost. The funds will then be included in the next funding or appropriation bill—a bill that may not appear for six months. This process, from planning to costing to funding, often takes a couple of years before the funds are available for obligation. Some of this time lag is the result of safeguards built into the funding cycle to protect against fraud. The problem is that the preferred technology may have changed during this time. The second problem is that the government salary structure limits the government's ability to hire the best technology experts. The bottom line is substantial thought, and planning must go into development and implementation of the technology.

- **Policy experts.** These individuals will ensure that the implementation is consistent with both the language and the intent of the legislation. Policy experts are typically individuals who have worked on congressional committees, pulling together the legislation. The legislative language is critical because there are times when congressional intent was not captured; thus, this additional expertise can be helpful.

Develop the Plan

The implementation plan and timeline should be a working document that lists the milestones, activities, responsible parties and estimated time for individual task execution. It may also include costs, expected obstacles and objectives, contractors to be used and outside groups to be briefed. This document should be continuously vetted and revised. It should also show potential dependencies among the various tasks and include default strategies.

This plan will continue to be revised, but when the draft plan is complete, it will be reviewed to flag the tasks with the greatest risks. Default or backup plans must then be created. All staff must feel comfortable raising objections to the plan and offering changes. The team must reach consensus on both the vision and the plan for implementation. If one or two staff members oppose the plan, it may be necessary to replace these individuals on the team.

Involve Stakeholders

Successful policy implementation in the United States requires public participation, where those who are implementing the policy are constantly engaged in a dialogue on all major issues. There are essentially two stakeholder groups. First are those industries or groups the policy will affect directly. Second, there is the general public.

For example, when Medicare Part D (the drug benefit) was enacted, every pharmaceutical company, physician, drug store and any other establishment that dispenses drugs was affected. In addition, Part D had a major effect on consumers of pharmaceuticals. Essentially, both of these groups were key to making the program successful because they are the essence of the private health care system in the United States. Ensuring that each sector can implement its responsibilities in a timely manner is critical and requires extensive briefings and some modification of the government's plan. Therefore, it is worth it to get buy-in from providers so that implementation is smooth.

The other major groups concerned with Part D consisted of the Medicare-eligible population, followed by the public at large. Public information campaigns had to be created to inform both populations. By and large, Part D was a massive implementation, but because of effective planning and communication, it was one that had a smooth implementation.

Create a Feedback Loop to Evaluate Progress and Results

Given the number of obstacles any implementation of a new law faces, many adjustments will be made to the plan and timeline over time. The staff must understand this early on and be flexible and adaptable. A formal process with three separate loops should be established to gather information. The first loop is continuous outreach to the stakeholders, which would include industry representatives and state and local governments. The next loop is outreach to citizens and potential consumers as well as the public at large. The final loop is a political check with Congress or the affected state legislatures. After a detailed evaluation of the information, adjustment to the plan or timeline may be necessary. Care must be taken, however, to differentiate between clear problems and general complaints.

Chapter 9
A Final Comment

This guide has provided a detailed overview on how to write a public policy capstone paper. As such it has focused primarily on how to make estimates of the various concepts that are critical to the underlying analytical foundation. The goal is to write an analytical not a descriptive paper. Throughout the guide it has highlighted several major themes that are critical to the evaluation of any public policy issue. It shows how to integrate the processes for financing programs as part of the analysis of alternative policies. It also demonstrates the importance of policy implementation and how it must be integrated into the policy development process from the beginning. Further, it stresses the importance of combining data analysis with the advice of individuals who have substantial expertise with the issue. These can be academics, individuals involved in administering similar programs, or even some who have been enrolled in a program.

Moving forward, it is important to keep an eye on several trends that have emerged over the past five to ten years that are affecting the role of analysis in public policy decisions. The first is that the political climate has become highly partisan, from the local school board to the state legislatures to the U.S. Congress. Partisan politics has affected the policies adopted at all levels of government. In conservative states, policies have drifted to the right; in progressive states, they have drifted to the left. Neither policy direction is good for the American people.

When the two parties get together, the consensus can lead to adoption of more middle-of-the-road policies that receive broader support from the electorate, which in turn enhances trust in government. It is also true that the lack of sustainability of laws, regulations and court decisions is a growing concern for all governments because too much energy is spent attempting to repeal policies enacted by the other party. The best example of this effect was the aftermath of the enactment of the Patient Protection and Affordable Care Act in 2010. The Democrats passed the bill without any Republican support, as witnessed by the fact that no Republican in either the House or Senate voted for the final bill. What followed was nearly a decade of Republicans attempting to either repeal the act in the Congress or have it declared unconstitutional by the U.S. Supreme Court.

Several years later, following the election of Donald Trump and the Republicans gaining a majority in both houses of Congress, the GOP used the same tactic to enact the Tax Cuts and Jobs Act of 2017. No Democrats voted for this bill, and if the Democrats had a larger majority in the Senate under the Biden administration, they would have attempted to repeal many of the tax cuts, particularly for higher-income individuals. Both parties are to blame for these partisan actions. The unfortunate fallout is a second trend which is increased uncertainty to both citizens and businesses regarding the sustainability of policies. This uncertainty leads to lower levels of investment and productivity which in turn negatively impacts economic growth. Finally, both the increased partisanship and uncertainty lowers trust in government, which affects all facets of our democracy.

Regardless of these troubling trends analysts should not change their approach. They must stay the course in terms of their analytical approach and dependence on, data and evidence as well as their objectivity and transparency.

Appendix A
Choosing the Topic

Clearly, there is an interdependence between the client and your topic, which raises the question: Should you choose the client first, and then hope that you can negotiate a topic of interest? Or should you decide on the topic first, and then shop it to potential clients?

Go with Passion

Which route you choose depends on the level of passion you have for the topic. If it is high, I recommend specifying the topic, and then contacting several potential clients to find one willing to be a sponsor. Remember that you will be working on this issue over two semesters, which is a long time. Therefore, it is important that you enjoy the topic to help maintain your motivation.

Selection of a topic and client could also be the first step in deciding on future employment. Many employers today ask for an example of a student's work, so the capstone report is an ideal example of an in-depth analytical paper. Over these couple of semesters, you will get to know your client and the other Individuals who provided advice on your topic. Think of this group as the beginning of a professional network, which is important for long-term career success.

Keep the Topic Narrow

One of the comments I hear most often from students, toward the end of the course, is that their topic was so large it overwhelmed them. I recommend that you choose a narrowly defined problem. The potential depth is more important than its breadth. Rather than a problem such as lack of access to health care in the United States, it might be better to focus on lack of access for families under 100% of poverty or lack of access for Black or Hispanic families. Alternatively, restrict your analysis to a city or state. A broad topic in combination with a large geographic region, such as the entire United States, can be all consuming. Narrowly defined topics and regions enable you to conduct a more in-depth analysis, which often leads to more enjoyable work and a better outcome.

Check the Data

Another major frustration that students experience toward the end of the first semester is a lack of data available to measure cost-effectiveness. When this happens, the final report becomes much more qualitative and descriptive, and the student fails to develop the important skill of how to use data. Therefore, before finalizing your topic, determine whether sufficient historical data exist on the outcomes, outputs and potential costs. Regardless of how robust the data are, you will have to make many assumptions. Although such assumptions are acceptable, lack of historical data substantially reduces the quality of the final report.

Select the Best Level of Government

After you decide on the general area of interest or topic, the next decision is what level of government you will focus on. Remember that all three levels of government have a role in most domestic issues—federal, state and local. Choose the level of government that has the greatest number of domestic policy levers. This choice is not necessarily obvious, however, and may require some research.

If national defense is your passion, then focus on the federal government. State and local government have few policy levers in that space. If your interest is in higher education, choose states. For elementary and secondary education, your focus could be state or local government, the school districts or even an individual school. Housing generally falls under the jurisdiction of local government. For health care, the focus could be the federal government, but states have large roles in areas such as administering Medicaid and the State Children's Health Insurance Program. States also have a major role in overseeing malpractice, scope of practice and health insurance regulations; as well as administering marketplace exchanges; and certifying physicians and nurse practitioners. Public health, in contrast, is most often a local government responsibility. Many environmental issues, such as clean air, are primarily a federal responsibility, but they are increasingly becoming a state responsibility. Students who choose a project on air pollution for a local government will often be frustrated by the lack of policy options.

Choose Greater Political Impact

On balance, the lower the level of government, the greater the potential for actual political impact. It is difficult for a capstone report to have an impact on the decisions of a federal agency or Congress: There is just too much competition. There are many cases, however, where a capstone recommendation has been discussed in a city council meeting or state legislature hearing. Essentially, the smaller the government, the greater the interest in the paper and the greater the potential impact.

Appendix B
Creating a Mud Hut of Advisers

During the 27 years I ran the National Governors Association (NGA), I learned a great deal about politics and policy, but one experience stands out. In 1986–87, when Arkansas Gov. Bill Clinton became the NGA chair, I made several trips to Little Rock to brief him on the progress of his major initiative, called "Making America Work," and to talk about the status of the association's major legislative initiatives. During those trips, he often asked me to tag along when he was speaking to a community organization. Although the speeches were interesting, the more educational moments were when he would have his driver stop at a school or welfare office on the way to the speech or back to the Capitol. He would talk to the school principal, but he was always more interested in talking to the students, the teachers and the school secretaries. Similarly, if it was an intake office where individuals were filling out forms to determine their eligibility for welfare, he would talk to the office director and staff but usually spent more time with those individuals applying for welfare benefits. I witnessed a similar preference when I recommended that a panel of academics who had written extensively on welfare-to-work present at the winter meeting in Washington, D.C., where 49 of the 50 governors would be in attendance. He pushed back on my recommendation and said, "What would the governors learn from that session?" He had already decided to invite several women from Arkansas who had been on welfare but with the help of the state had received education, job training and child care assistance and thus found good-paying jobs and left the welfare rolls. It was a fascinating session. Both experiences taught me a simple lesson: You can learn a great deal from the staff at all levels who administer programs as well as those enrolled in a program.

Based on this experience, I have three recommendations. First, early in the project, find one or two individuals who are currently working in the program you are evaluating with whom you can check-in with every few weeks for advice on emerging problems and potential solutions. Often, staff at intermediate levels may be more accessible than office directors or other senior staff. Second, find several academics who have studied and written on your issue with whom you can check in, particularly early in your research, or who can help you connect with other knowledgeable individuals when you have developed your preliminary recommendations. Finally, do not forget individuals who are enrolled in or have participated in the program you are researching. This entire group, if used correctly, will evolve into a mud hut of advisers. The best capstone reports are produced by those students with one foot in the ivory tower, where data and analysis are key and the other with the mud hut of advisors.

Appendix C
Choosing and Working
with a Client

As described in Appendix A, if you have real passion for a particular topic, then it is typically best to start developing the topic before shopping it to potential clients. Otherwise, it may be better to choose a client first. The best clients are those who have both political and policy credibility on the issue. Such a client can be particularly helpful in opening doors to other experts, be they academic experts or individuals currently administering similar programs.

Research potential clients before you decide which to approach for sponsorship. The best options for clients are individuals working at any government agency or even some quasi-governmental agency. Alternatively, many nonprofit organizations or 501(c)3 entities will be good clients. It should be up to the school to decide whether a for-profit organization or any entity affiliated with the college or university is an acceptable client. My experience with for-profit organizations has not been positive, but their roles are clearly changing. Often, friends and parents can be helpful in contacting a potential client, but cold emails or calls can also be successful. Contacting staff at the intermediate level may be the most productive approach because they have knowledge and may be more willing to help.

Send a Letter of Confirmation

When you have a verbal agreement with a client, it is important that the individual receive a formal letter from the college or university that describes your and the client's responsibilities. It is critical that the client understand that the school, and thus the supervising professor, have requirements in terms of the definition of the problem and the definition of the outcome that may not be negotiable. Do not sign off on these definitions before consulting you professor. The letter should also stress that the study must be objective and analytical.

Determine Communication

During the early part of the relationship with the client, determine how often the client would like to be briefed and whether the client would like to approve the final report before you submit it. It is often beneficial to create several short progress reports during the semester, even if the client also wants a verbal briefing. The combination of a written report that you can share with other individuals who work with the client and an oral briefing is always good. Some individuals prefer to read, while others prefer to listen. Increasingly, politicians have limited time and thus prefer an oral briefing. During your discussions, see if the client is willing to appoint two additional contacts, even if they are both backups. It is surprising how many clients are either promoted or accept another job during a student's capstone, and then that student may completely lose the client.

Indicate Flexibility

Be flexible on incorporating the client's preferred policy option into your analysis. Some clients already have a preferred option and would like you to confirm it in your analysis. Obviously, you cannot do that, but it is fine to include it: Just be sure to indicate that the client's preferred approach may not be the right one. Also, the client may be willing to accept an in-depth technical report but has more interest in a different paper. For example, the client may want a lobbying strategy or a Microsoft PowerPoint presentation or a decision memo. You can easily include these as an appendix to the report or in a separate report. After you write the large technical report, you become an expert on your topic, making it relatively easy to complete other high-priority papers.

Send a Thank-You Note at the End

Always write a final thank-you letter to the client to show your appreciation. Remember that many clients take on this role as their contribution to society, and many spend numerous hours on the initiative.

Appendix D
A Checklist for the Final Report

The twenty-five issues addressed in this list are small, but making sure that they are correct adds to the professional look and feel of your capstone report:

- The executive summary should be short-no more than a page. It should define the problem, provide context, and then give key findings and recommendations. It is not necessary to include all criteria and alternatives.

- In general, students often choose to have heading like "Background" or "Literature Review."
  This is not the best approach as each heading should be short and indicate to the reader what is coming (e.g., "The Structure of the Electricity Market"). It is also best to use several subheads—again, they tell the reader what is coming and create some white space for ease of reading. They also help you make sure that everything written under a subhead is consistent with the subhead.

- Make sure each table, chart and figure is numbered and has a title and a source. Label each axis, column and row, as appropriate. Always refer to the critical statistic in the table or figure—for example, "as you can see in Table 2, the cost of health care in the United States is about twice that of the average Organization for Economic Cooperation and Development country." Reports can be improved with several graphs and tables, but do not go overboard just to fill space.

- The costs-to-society discussion should include both direct spending and the loss in wages and economic output as well as the cost of externalities. It should have a bottom line in terms of a point or range of estimates.

- Round numbers in the text to millions or billions. For example, use "$10 million" rather than "$10,000,000."

- For federal, state and local budgets, use the most recent actual spending, expenditures or outlays. Appropriations, obligations, budget authority and proposed budgets are not useful measures, especially for calculating cost-effectiveness.

- Create a one-page acknowledgement that describes and thanks the client. Do not talk about the client elsewhere in the report.

- Each alternative should be a specific proposal, not a conceptual discussion. For example, if you are proposing a tax incentive, that proposal should indicate the type of equipment eligible, the percentage that is a credit, the dollar cap and whether it is refundable. Include sufficient detail to establish a cost for the alternative.

- Use statistics and data to back up major points. In general, give absolute numbers and percentage changes—for example, "because of the COVID-19 pandemic, state revenues fell from $100 million to $50 million, a 50% reduction from the second quarter of 2019 to the second quarter of 2020."
- When there are several bullets, make sure they are all consistent, for example, all start with action verbs.

An Example for policy alternatives:

- Alternative 1. Continue the current policy.
- Alternative 2. Impose a new fee of $20.00 per ton on carbon dioxide emissions.
- Alternative 3. Adopt a new regulation to allow net metering.
- When you use statistics to emphasize a point, they should always come from the primary source, such as a federal government agency (e.g., U.S. Census Bureau, the U.S. Department of Labor). Avoid taking data from a newspaper or research entity.
- To the extent possible, base your analysis on peer-reviewed articles as they are the most credible sources.
- Describe your methodology for calculating cost-effectiveness in the final report. For a good example, see Table 21.1 in the article by Cellini

and Kee[28] for a good summary of the concepts, assumptions and final estimates. A more detailed methodology and any spread sheets should be in an appendix.

o Number all pages.

o Avoid general statements, such as "It grew rapidly." Say instead, "It grew from 50 to 100, a 100% increase from 2009 to 2018."

o For gross domestic product and other economic variables, be clear if it is in nominal or real dollars.

o Do not give hints about or foreshadow your findings and recommendation.

o 18. Maps can be helpful, but label and reference them as you would a figure or table.

o Keep your report to 10,000 words (not including appendices). Just before submission, edit the report several times to make sure it reads well. Take a couple of days break from the report in between these editing rounds.

o Students tend to be vague in their writing. Fight that tendency: Always be as specific as possible.

o White space is important because dense writing and long paragraphs put readers off. Look at

---

[28] Riegg Cellini, S., and Kee, J. E. (2015). Cost-effectiveness and cost-benefit analysis. In Wholey, J. S., Hatry, H. P., and Newcomer, K. E. (Eds.), *Handbook of practical program evaluation.* (3rd ed., pp. 493–530). Wiley.

each page: How can you cut words, shorten sentences and add white space?

o   Avoid jargon and overly technical language. You are writing your report for a lay audience.

o   Make sure formatting and headings are consistent throughout the paper.

o   Look to the American Psychological Association for guidance on citations.

o   Submit your capstone report before the deadline.

Appendix E
Federal-State Implementation

This guide has stressed the fact that implementation is a critical component of public policy and is often an afterthought. It is particularly challenging when the legislation is enacted by the federal government but the implementation is by state governments. That said, what follows is an example of a well-coordinated very successful federal/state implementation.

Federal-State Coordination of the American Recovery Act During the Great Recession of 2008–9

The Great Recession of 2008–9 was not your average cyclical economic downturn. Instead, it was a financial meltdown that caused Gross Domestic Product to experience four quarters of negative growth, from –2.75% in the last quarter of 2008 to –3.92% in the third quarter of 2009. Similarly, unemployment exploded during this period, reaching 9.9% in the last quarter of 2009.

Because of the seriousness of the downturn, then-President George W. Bush signed the Troubled Asset Relief Program (TARP) legislation on Oct. 3, 2008, to purchase financial assets and stabilize the U.S. financial system. TARP was followed by the enactment of the American Recovery and Reinvestment Act (ARRA) of 2009, which was signed into law by then-President Barack Obama on Feb. 17, 2009. The purpose of ARRA was to preserve and create jobs and promote economic recovery. The act included an estimated $787 billion in tax cuts and increased spending, of which about $300 billion went to state and local governments. That $300 billion was intended by the U.S. Congress not only to help stabilize state and local governments' fiscal position but, more importantly, to lessen potential tax increases and spending reductions that states and localities would be forced to make to meet their balanced-budget requirements. Congress believed that such austerity actions would only make the downturn more severe.

The additional federal funds ARRA provided to state and local governments were to be spent mostly in existing programs to avoid the time-consuming necessity of new rules and regulations, which would slow spending. States and localities were to spend the additional funds as quickly as possible while following all the existing guidelines for the programs ARRA authorized.

It is not uncommon for the U.S. economy to witness economic downturns, where Congress enacts different policies to minimize the impact on individuals. Therefore, it is important to look back over the last big stimulus to see what we learned. There are clear lessons regarding the structure and timing of the initiative, but this overview focuses on the implementation—more specifically, on the federal-state coordination of the $300 billion in aid to state and local governments. Most politicians and policy experts focus on the structure of the policy, but history tells us that public policies most often fail because of flawed implementation. Thus, there is much to learn from a look back at the implementation of ARRA.

1. The Goals and Tone Were Set by the Highest Elected Officials Early in the Process

President-elect Obama and Vice-President-elect Joseph Biden invited the 50 state governors to a meeting at Independence Hall in Philadelphia on Dec. 2, 2008, before the inauguration. Here, the president-elect asked for recommendations from the governors regarding state programs that could use additional funds during the downturn. Such a request helped the governors take ownership of the final bill, which included many of their recommendations. Obama indicated that the goal was to create 2.5 million jobs as quickly as possible. He was clear that he wanted to create a strong federal-state partnership in the implementation of this initiative. He also quoted U.S. Supreme Court Justice Louis Brandeis regarding states being the "laboratories of democracy." Essentially, Obama wanted states to experiment and be innovative in their approach to spending the funds. Although he emphasized spending the funds as quickly as possible, he also stressed transparency and accountability. Finally, he indicated that some of the funds were to create a foundation for longer-term growth. The involvement of the elected officials continued after the meeting, as the vice president and the governors had conference calls throughout the implementation period and the vice president hosted two Washington, D.C., meetings for state staff.

2. Several Informal and Flexible Working Groups with Specific Missions Were Created

The elected officials' group, which included the vice president and the 50 governors, was created to resolve major issues and share information. A worker bee group made up of federal and state staff coordinated on a day-to-day basis to share new information quickly and identify obstacles. A third group, which audited spending, watched for potential fraud and promoted transparency, was referred to as the "accountability group" and included staff members from the Government Accountability Office (GAO), the Recovery Accountability and Transparency Board (RAT Board), which included inspectors general of the key agencies, and representatives from the state and local audit community.

The Elected Officials Group. At least twice a month, the vice president would reach out to governors and other elected officials. These phone calls and occasional meetings gave the officials a chance to let the vice president know directly about any problems or concerns they had. As concerns were voiced, Vice President Biden instructed staff to resolve the matter and report to him within 24 hours. All issues were resolved within this time frame. Biden also used the calls to urge the officials to act in areas where spending was lagging. For example, applications for additional wastewater funds from the U.S. Environmental Protection Agency (EPA) were lagging, and ARRA placed a deadline on using or losing these funds. Last-minute calls from the vice president directly to governors helped ensure that the deadline was met.

Worker Bee Group. This group consisted of the budget officers of the 50 states; some National Governors Association (NGA) and National Association of State Budget Officers staff; and staff from the Office of Management and Budget (OMB), which was the lead agency for the administration. This group held weekly conference calls to share information and identify obstacles to spending the funds quickly or ensuring full transparency. When a problem was identified, it was quickly referred to an ad hoc group to be solved. Much of the conversation here involved state staff getting questions answered by OMB staff regarding the timing of when funds would become available or technical questions regarding how the funds were to be spent. Over time, staff from the GAO participated in the calls, where they would talk about problems they were seeing in some states regarding accountability.

Accountability Group. This group, which consisted of the RAT Board; the GAO; relevant inspectors general; and state and local auditors, controllers and treasurers, routinely met to coordinate work and compare findings. The RAT Board was composed of the inspectors general from each major agency receiving funds under ARRA. The RAT Board had a budget of $50 million to create and operate a data-collection system to meet statutory requirements for quarterly reporting of spending and performance. The system was modeled after one used in the EPA for grant reporting and featured more than 90 data elements. Reporting took place at the grantee level, with more than 75,000 grantees ultimately reporting. A key feature of the system was the geospatial character of the data. The RAT Board created a mapping system that allowed the public to see what was being spent and how many jobs were created in a particular area. The data were reported directly to the RAT Board, which was responsible for data integrity.

Of the several roles ARRA specified for the GAO, the most significant was conducting bimonthly reviews of select states' and localities' use of funds made available under the act. GAO embedded teams in 16 states and the District of Columbia and covered 60 localities within those 16 states. Every other month, the GAO provided ongoing longitudinal reports that analyzed approximately $200 billion, or about two-thirds of ARRA funds for states and localities. Those 16 states also covered about two-thirds of the U.S. population.

To do this, the GAO worked closely with governors' offices; "recovery czars"; state auditors, controllers and treasurers; and state and local program staff to evaluate the use of, accountability for and impact of ARRA funds. Such interactions were iterative, with the GAO giving real-time feedback about what it was finding, thereby giving states and localities the opportunity for timely midcourse corrections and the GAO the ability to fact check its work in near-real time. This quick turn required replacing the typical audit role of providing after-the-fact critiques with constructive engagement aimed at improving the ongoing implementation.

At a time of critical national importance, when time was of the essence and activity under scrutiny, such oversight not only evaluated but facilitated implementation, as auditors constructively engaged with those implementing programs, gave immediate feedback and enhanced communication across levels of government and functions.

3. A Free Flow of Information Across All Three Working Groups Was Developed

This free flow of information meant the worker bees could listen in on the conference calls between the vice president and the 50 governors, and members of the accountability team could participate in the weekly worker bee conference calls. It also meant that any interested staff member could participate in the conference calls of the ad hoc groups. Over time, all members involved in the coordination had access to almost any meeting or conference call, helping ensure that virtually everyone knew the status of every issue in real time.

4. Ad Hoc Groups of State Budget Directors, Federal Agency Staff and Office of Management and Budget Staff Were Created to Eliminate Obstacles Quickly

Obstacles often arose because of differences in interpretation in the federal rules that governed spending. Thus, it was necessary to get the three groups together to work through the problem. Sometimes, the problem was the interpretation of a so-called "maintenance-of-effort" rule or law, which generally indicated that a state needed to continue to spend from its own funds, a least at the same level as a given previous year. This was a particular issue for some education funds. Other times, such as with the weatherization program, the problem was just trying to determine why spending was so slow. Still other times, the issue might be whether the Davis-Bacon Act applied for certain construction projects. If these obstacles were serious, staff would ask governors to flag them for the vice president on the next call so that they would receive attention at the highest level.

5. The Accountability Group Operated in Parallel with the Two Operations Groups Instead of After the Fact

As noted, ARRA required the accountability community to replace its usual business model with one better suited to responding to the exigencies of the worst economic downturn since the Great Depression. In short, auditors needed to report quickly and generate accurate reports. The only way to do this was to network with others in the accountability community and those providing the auditors with their data.

The RAT Board, with its ever-growing database, and the GAO, with its legislatively required real-time reporting, formed the hub of a network that included inspectors general and state auditors, controllers and treasurers. This network engaged with states and localities charged with reporting on the funds they were receiving. With a database that was evolving as more data came in and with audits conducted under tight time frames and high scrutiny, it was essential that everyone was working with data that were accurate and consistent. The RAT Board and OMB tried to develop clear guidance, and state and local recipients tried to follow that guidance. The GAO and other auditors used the data but also noted where breakdowns occurred.

The network was most effective when continuous communication enabled recipients to provide direct feedback on what was or was not working, OMB and the RAT Board showed openness to making necessary changes and the auditors provided timely reality checks. The result was a database where the public could see, often down to the neighborhood level, what funds had been provided, how much had been spent, for what purpose and to what end. The auditors provided context for and confidence in these numbers. This bright light of transparency was aimed at making ARRA both real and trusted.

The three authors of this Appendix include myself, Raymond Scheppach, executive director of the NGA during this coordination and now retired professor of public policy at the University of Virginia Frank Batten School of Leadership and Public Policy. Stan Czerwinski was the

GAO director for state and local governments during ARRA implementation. Edward DeSeve has held so many luminous positions it would take too long to list them but at the time was the OMB lead who reported directly to Vice President Biden.